365 IDEAS

for Recruiting, Retaining, Motivating and Rewarding Your Volunteers:

A Complete Guide for Nonprofit Organizations

Revised 2nd Edition

First Edition by: Sunny Fader

Revised by: Angela Erickson

D0721850

365 IDEAS FOR RECRUITING, RETAINING, MOTIVATING AND REWARDING YOUR VOLUNTEERS: A COMPLETE GUIDE FOR NONPROFIT ORGANIZATIONS - REVISED 2ND EDITION

Copyright © 2017 Atlantic Publishing Group, Inc.
1405 SW 6th Avenue • Ocala, Florida 34471 • Phone 800-814-1132 • Fax 352-622-1875
Website: www.atlantic-pub.com • Email: sales@atlantic-pub.com
SAN Number: 268-1250

No part of this publication may be reproduced, stored in a retrieval system, or transmitted in any form or by any means, electronic, mechanical, photocopying, recording, scanning, or otherwise, except as permitted under Section 107 or 108 of the 1976 United States Copyright Act, without the prior written permission of the Publisher. Requests to the Publisher for permission should be sent to Atlantic Publishing Group, Inc., 1405 SW 6th Avenue, Ocala, Florida 34471.

Library of Congress Cataloging-in-Publication Data

Names: Fader, Sunny, 1931- author.
Title: 365 ideas for recruiting, retaining, motivating and rewarding your
  volunteers : a complete guide for nonprofit organizations / Sunny Fader.
Other titles: Three hundred sixty-five ideas for recruiting, retaining,
  motivating, and rewarding your volunteers
Description: Revised 2nd Edition. | Ocala : Atlantic Publishing Group, Inc.,
  [2017] | Revised edition of the author's 365 ideas for recruiting,
  retaining, motivating, and rewarding your volunteers, c2010. | Includes
  bibliographical references and index.
Identifiers: LCCN 2016046563 (print) | LCCN 2016049051 (ebook) | ISBN
  9781620230589(alk.paper) | ISBN 1620230747 (alk. paper) | ISBN
  9781620230749 (ebook)
Subjects: LCSH: Volunteers--Recruiting. | Nonprofit
  organizations--Employees--Recruiting.
Classification: LCC HD8039.N65 F33 2017 (print) | LCC HD8039.N65 (ebook) |
  DDC 658.3--dc23
LC record available at https://lccn.loc.gov/2016046563

LIMIT OF LIABILITY/DISCLAIMER OF WARRANTY: The publisher and the author make no representations or warranties with respect to the accuracy or completeness of the contents of this work and specifically disclaim all warranties, including without limitation warranties of fitness for a particular purpose. No warranty may be created or extended by sales or promotional materials. The fact that an organization or website is referred to in this work as a citation and/or a potential source of further information does not mean that the author or the publisher endorses the information the organization or websites may provide or recommendations it may make. Further, readers should be aware that internet websites listed in this work may have changed or disappeared between when this work was written and when it is read.

Disclaimer: The author has made every effort to ensure the accuracy of the information within this book was correct at time of publication. The author does not assume and hereby disclaims any liability to any party for any loss, damage, or disruption caused by errors or omissions, whether such errors or omissions result from accident, negligence, or any other cause.

Printed in the United States

PROJECT MANAGER AND EDITOR: Rebekah Sack • rsack@atlantic-pub.com
INTERIOR LAYOUT: Justin Oefelein • justin.o@spxmultimedia.com
COVER DESIGN: Jackie Miller • millerjackiej@gmail.com
JACKET DESIGN: Antoinette D Amore • addesign@videotron.ca

Reduce. Reuse.
RECYCLE.

A decade ago, Atlantic Publishing signed the Green Press Initiative. These guidelines promote environmentally friendly practices, such as using recycled stock and vegetable-based inks, avoiding waste, choosing energy-efficient resources, and promoting a no-pulping policy. We now use 100-percent recycled stock on all our books. The results: in one year, switching to post-consumer recycled stock saved 24 mature trees, 5,000 gallons of water, the equivalent of the total energy used for one home in a year, and the equivalent of the greenhouse gases from one car driven for a year.

Over the years, we have adopted a number of dogs from rescues and shelters. First there was Bear and after he passed, Ginger and Scout. Now, we have Kira, another rescue. They have brought immense joy and love not just into our lives, but into the lives of all who met them.

We want you to know a portion of the profits of this book will be donated in Bear, Ginger and Scout's memory to local animal shelters, parks, conservation organizations, and other individuals and nonprofit organizations in need of assistance.

– Douglas & Sherri Brown,
President & Vice-President of Atlantic Publishing

Table of Contents

A Word from the Author

I have spent a good portion of my life involved in the not-for-profit arena, both professionally and personally, so it did not surprise me when so many nonprofit organizations responded to my request for stories illustrating successful policies or innovative ideas that have helped them recruit and motivate their volunteers. People who work in this area are, by nature, generous with their help. I was, however, unprepared for the great diversity in size and focus represented in these responses.

I heard from a well-known international group that fights poverty on another continent and a neighborhood soup kitchen that fights that same battle in its own backyard. Emails came in from well-funded, well-staffed foundations working to end various diseases and from a woman in Michigan who has managed to harness the power of local volunteer quilters to raise awareness and money for research on Alzheimer's disease. There was a man in Illinois who trains volunteers of all ages to respond to disasters and emergencies in their small town, and a national agency that draws upon volunteers nationwide to help in the aftermath of major disasters. In the area of the arts, I heard from museums, community theaters, and orchestras.

I deeply appreciate the time these individuals and so many others have taken from their busy schedules to help me with this book. Because of the great diversity in size, focus, and resources they represent, you may find some of the experiences they have shared here are not applicable to your particular circumstances. However, it is my hope that the sound philosophies behind their experiences and the innovative approaches they have taken will inspire you to expand your vision and encourage you to explore new ideas so you can breathe new life into your own volunteer program.

Sunny Fader

Introduction

Regardless of their size or focus, organizations that operate under the nonprofit banner face the same challenge: how to find enough money and enough people to do all that needs to be done. Because the financial health of a nonprofit depends heavily on the generosity of strangers, finding enough money will always be a challenge — even in the best of times — but finding enough people does not have to be. *365 Ideas for Recruiting, Retaining, Motivating, and Rewarding Your Volunteers* is, as its subtitle indicates, *A Complete Guide for Nonprofit Organizations* — a tool that can help you not only find, but keep the volunteers that are essential to your ability to carry out your mission.

Having a reliable corps of volunteers is always a good thing, but today it is crucial. In March of 2015 the Nonprofit Finance Fund (NFF) surveyed 5,451 nonprofit professionals to discover what effect the recent economic downturn was having on their organizations. Its findings confirmed what anyone working for a nonprofit already knew: this country's 1.5 million nonprofit organizations are experiencing a serious erosion of resources. Donations are down. Grants are becoming more difficult to find. The flagging economy has even affected that most reliable of nonprofit resources, the endowment, diminishing many and, in some cases, wiping them out altogether. Some interesting figures were revealed in this study: 76 percent of nonprofits reported an increase in demand for services — the seventh year that a majority have reported increases. 52 percent couldn't meet demand — the third year in a row that more than half of nonprofits couldn't meet demand. Of those who reported that they could not meet demand, **71 percent said that client needs go unmet when they can't provide services.**

As a result, many nonprofit organizations are being forced to take drastic steps to survive. They are eliminating valuable programs and cutting staff — two actions that make having a reliable volunteer program in place more important than ever. Before we explore how to create such a program, there are three myths concerning volunteers that need to be addressed.

MYTH #1: THERE IS A SHORTAGE OF POTENTIAL VOLUNTEERS

The statistical background: According to the Corporation for National and Community Service, in 2013 62.6 million Americans — 25.4 percent of the adult population — contributed 7.7 billion hours of volunteer service to various organizations. But while the size of this volunteer pool has remained relatively stable the past few years, the number of nonprofits competing for this limited pool continues to grow.

On the surface, the statistics are discouraging: a growing number of financially stressed nonprofits all competing for a limited pool of available volunteers. But let us view the situation from a different perspective.

Some years ago, a man with a heart for ministry and a gift for communicating had a unique concept for a public relations company. His name was Russ Reid, and he created a marketing firm that works exclusively for nonprofits and faith-based organizations serving worthy causes – organizations that fight hunger and disease, or reach out to serve at risk populations. Over the years this agency has created successful direct mail campaigns and television fundraising specials for such organizations as World Vision, the Los Angeles Mission^SM, the American Cancer Society®, and St. Jude Children's Research Hospital. The key to the agency's success can be found in Russ Reid's philosophy about fundraising. He believed people have a built-in need to give. All you have to do is make them comfortable giving to your organization.

This insight does not only apply to the giving of money, it also applies to our intrinsic need to give of ourselves — to contribute our time and our gifts to the ongoing quest to make our world safer, kinder, or more beautiful. From this perspective, there is no shortage of potential volunteers. There is a vast, untapped source of them, waiting to serve — if only someone would take the trouble to ask them. All you have to do to tap into their need is find a way to make them feel comfortable sharing their time and talents with your organization. This same philosophy applies to the next myth.

MYTH #2: VOLUNTEERS ARE DIFFICULT TO KEEP

The statistical background: According to the Corporation for National and Community Service, only 63.5 percent of the volunteers who served in 2009 returned to service again in 2010.

While this trend in disturbing, you have the power to make your organization the exception to the rule. People's circumstances change. When you are dealing with volunteers, some attrition is to be expected. But if you create a welcoming, friendly atmosphere for your volunteers and succeed in making them comfortable investing their talents and time in your cause, you will eliminate the major reason most volunteers stop working for an organization.

MYTH #3: VOLUNTEERS ARE FREE

The reasoning behind the myth: Because volunteers are not paid, their services do not cost a nonprofit anything.

The use of volunteers can be cost effective, but it is not cost free. Before we discuss the cost, let us look at the value volunteers bring to your organization. According to the Independent Sector website, the estimated dollar value put on a volunteer's time in 2010 was $21.36 an hour. Even when ignoring the other benefits volunteers offer, this figure establishes the fact volunteers are worth something and that they have real value. Of course a nonprofit does not pay their volunteers this amount — or for that matter, anything at all — but that does not mean their services are free.

Like any valuable asset, volunteers require maintenance and supervision. This necessitates an investment of staff time for which the nonprofit does have to pay. Then there is the cost involved in the recruiting process, as well as insurance and legal fees. If you want an effective team of volunteers, you are also going to have to invest in training for them, and some kind of reward or recognition program. In other words, while you may not pay your volunteers, they will require a financial and time investment. But considering the value they bring to your organization, you will receive an excellent return on your investment.

With these myths out of the way, you are now ready to explore the 365 ideas for recruiting, retaining, motivating, and rewarding your volunteers and the other information presented in this book. You will also meet some colleagues who will share with you some of the successful philosophies and innovative concepts they have found helpful in their work with volunteers. Also included in this updated version are new statistics for research regarding volunteers, as well as more discussion on the topic of social media and technology in today's modern world. Whether you choose to apply these ideas or concepts directly or glean inspiration from them, it is our hope that this book will help you develop a dynamic, motivated, reliable team of volunteers for your nonprofit organization.

CHAPTER 1:

BEFORE YOU BEGIN RECRUITING

A motivated, reliable team of volunteers is not something that just happens. It is the product of a focused, well-planned recruitment effort. Recruiting is the key to an effective volunteer program because how you recruit your volunteers affects the kind of relationship you are going to have with them. The way you tell your story, define your needs, and relate what the volunteer experience will be like in your organization creates certain expectations in the minds of your candidates. According to research, one of the principal reasons volunteers leave an organization is because their experience with the nonprofit failed to live up to their expectations.

RECRUITMENT PREPARATION CHECKLIST

☑ Determine your needs

☑ Analyze workspace

☑ Select volunteer liaison

☑ Prepare budget

☑ Involve board members

☑ Prepare staff

☑ Legal & safety considerations

☑ Screening policy & questionnaire

☑ Design a user-friendly record-keeping system

The time to address this potential problem is during recruiting by being clear about your organization's needs and by providing potential volunteers with an opportunity to discuss their needs and expectations with you. In doing this you take a major step toward ensuring your volunteers' involvement with your organization will be a positive experience. First, however, you must determine what your needs are.

Determining Needs

Your needs will depend on the nature of your organization. Here are a few things you might want to consider:

- Do you need volunteers to support your paid office staff? Are there routine tasks such as filing or computer input a volunteer could do that would free your staff for more urgent work?

- Will your volunteers be working out in the field with clients or on other kinds of projects? Will they need any special protective clothing or equipment to do the job?

- Do you have a need for volunteers with computer skills or other technical capabilities?

- Are you looking for help with fundraising? Will you need to provide these volunteers with special training? What kind of fundraising materials will they need?

- Will your volunteers interface with your clients? What characteristics or skills do you need to look for in these volunteers? What kind of training will they need?

- What resources will you need to have on hand for new volunteers, and who will be responsible for providing them?

A brainstorming session with your staff and board members will give you the most comprehensive view of your organization's needs. It will also help you evaluate whether, or what kind of, volunteers should be enlisted to fill these specific needs.

> "Recruiting is not simply the act of asking someone to volunteer or putting flyers at a local library. It is a multi-step process that builds to engagement."
> — *Great Expectations: Boomers and the Future of Volunteering*
> **VolunteerMatch 2007**

Analyzing Workspace Needs

Even if your volunteers will be working in another location, you will need a place in your office or central home base where they can report in and complete the paperwork connected with their jobs. Some points to consider are:

- What kind of space are you going to need?

- Can you dedicate a space for your volunteers, or are they going to have to share space with staff? If it is a shared space, can you work out a schedule for volunteer use of that space that will not disrupt your staff?

- Will your volunteers require any special equipment or furniture such as computers, filing cabinets, desks, or a coffee machine?

Choosing a Volunteer Liaison

Another critical piece you will want to have in place before you begin recruiting is a procedure for how your volunteers will interact with your staff. Even if you use a volunteer to coordinate volunteer activities, he or she will have to report to some staff member.

There are similarities between supervising employees and supervising volunteers. Both require organization and a clear chain of command. There is also one important difference: Employees do not have to like the person supervising them. They understand that they are there to do a job, for which they are getting paid. But if your volunteer does not find the experience of volunteering pleasurable, there is nothing to keep him or her from leaving. This makes the selection of a liaison to interface with, or supervise your volunteers, a critical decision that could mean the difference between whether those volunteers stay or leave.

Here are some things to consider when choosing a volunteer supervisor or staff liaison for your volunteers.

- Does the staff member you plan to designate have the personality and disposition to handle this responsibility? Are they pleasant, good communicators, and patient? Do they enjoy working with people and are they appreciative of the service volunteers perform?

- Would this individual do a better job if you invested in some training for him or her?

- Will this individual's workload interfere with his or her ability to fulfill the responsibilities of a volunteer liaison? Can it be adjusted to prevent this?

- If the liaison selected has a heavy workload, would it be feasible to restrict contact hours for volunteers?

- If your volunteers work during times your offices are closed, who will they contact in case of an emergency?

- Do you have a backup liaison if your appointed liaison is not available?

- If you are a volunteer-run nonprofit, do you have a backup for your volunteer liaison so your volunteers always have someone to contact for assignments or questions?

IN-KIND DONATION: Paid or given in goods, commodities, or services instead of money: *in-kind welfare programs.* (Dictionary.com)

Smaller institutions such as churches or community-based nonprofits with limited staffs may have little or no choice in who they can appoint as volunteer liaison. If you are not fortunate enough to have someone with the desired people skills to fill the post, with a little patience you can help whoever assumes the responsibility cultivate some of these skills. People can be taught to listen. They can also be taught to be patient and more thoughtful, and to remember to say thank you — all the little things that help to create a pleasant experience for volunteers.

Preparing a Recruitment Budget

No matter how many in-kind and donated services you get for your recruitment efforts, you are still going to incur some costs. It is better to plan for them up front and be pleasantly surprised if your campaign comes in under budget than to have to deal with the stress of trying to find money for commitments you made, but did not budget for. A prepared budget at this stage of the process also gives you something concrete to take to your board — a target figure to ask for.

Although it is always good to have a figure in mind, the amount you can spend on your recruitment campaign will ultimately be determined by your board, based on your organization's overall operational budget. This amount will vary from organization to organization. Do not be afraid to enlist help in putting your campaign budget together. You may have people on your staff, on your board, or among your volunteers whose skills at number-crunching or knowledge of the community can help you get the most value out of available recruitment funds.

If available, you can use budgets from past recruitment campaigns as a guideline, but each campaign should be looked at with fresh eyes. Communities change. You may discover new ways to get your message out that will affect how you decide to allocate your funds. Be sure to include a contingency figure in your budget to cover unexpected expenses.

Once you know how much you have to spend and have decided on the skills or type of volunteers you are looking for, you are ready to create your campaign budget. The sample budget form on the next page can serve as a model to help you create your own, more specific and detailed budget.

SAMPLE RECRUITMENT BUDGET FORM

Using the sample below, create your own form to plan and track recruitment expenses

Item	Amount budgeted	In-kind of donation	Actual cost	Comments
Office supplies.				
Paid print advertising				
Paid radio and tv promotion				
Stationery				
Banners				
Posters				
Promotional items				
Travel reimbursement				
Food costs				
Event expenses				
Contingency				
Total				

The Role of Your Board

The primary reason for including your board at the planning stage of your recruitment effort is that they are the ones who have the authority to allocate the money you will need for your project. There are, however, other reasons that are equally important.

- Board members have contacts that can help you get your recruitment message out into the community.

- Their contacts can also help you line up donations and in-kind services for your recruitment campaign.

- If you are looking for particular skills or talents such as accounting or computer skills, artists, or medical professionals, there is a good chance that out of the diversity of your board you will find someone who can connect you with potential volunteers who can meet your specific need.

- You may find skills on your board you can use directly in preparing for your recruitment effort — a board member with an advertising or promotion background, or accounting or bookkeeping skills to help in preparing the budget.

- The enthusiastic backing of your board from the beginning can inject energy into your project that will help move it forward.

Involving Your Staff

Whether they will interact directly or indirectly with new volunteers, staff members have much to contribute to the recruitment process. More than anyone, they know what is needed in the way of volunteers — where volunteer help would be most useful and where it might negatively impact

the staff's current workload (by taking them away from their own work). By listening to your staff and showing respect for their knowledge and their needs, you will also be taking a major step toward assuring a smooth transition when it comes time to bring the new volunteers onboard.

Legal and Safety Considerations

In planning your recruitment program, there are certain legal and safety requirements that must be taken into consideration, particularly when designing the volunteer screening portion of your program. These requirements or regulations are usually defined in an organization's risk management and liability reduction plan. These plans are designed to protect personnel and volunteers in the event of personal injury, loss of property, or a lawsuit; they also help ensure a safe environment for volunteers, employees, and clients that is free of predators or disruptive or unstable individuals.

Even small grassroots organization should have some kind of risk management and liability reduction policy in place before they begin recruiting. If your organization does not have a risk management and liability reduction plan, consult the bibliography for a list of websites that provide free help in setting up these programs.

While your organization's risk management and liability reduction plan must be a consideration in planning your recruitment effort, the complexity of your screening process' safety component depends on the nature of the work you will be asking your volunteers to perform. The more sensitive the volunteer assignments, the more thorough your screening process needs to be. If your volunteers will be working with children or other vulnerable populations, it would be prudent to include a police background check and questions designed to discover information pertaining to criminal records or legal problems. If the volunteers will be arranging cans of food at a food bank, a lesser degree of scrutiny might suffice.

Creating a Screening Policy and Questionnaire

The primary purpose of a volunteer screening policy is to help you find suitable volunteers for your organization. We will discuss the screening process in more detail in Chapter 6. Here we are concerned with how to prepare for the process.

Once you have determined the types of positions you want to fill and the skills or characteristics you are looking for in your new volunteers, you will have the information you need to create your volunteer questionnaire — a document you will give volunteer candidates to fill out at the beginning of the screening process. The purpose of the questionnaire is to learn about the candidate:

his or her personal background, education, interests, and any other information that will help you decide on the candidate's suitability for the volunteer positions you have available. For example, if the volunteer position involves helping with children or the elderly, you might want to include a question about the candidate's experiences with these populations. If you are looking for volunteers to help with computer input, you would ask about computer literacy. The completed questionnaire will provide the starting point for whoever will conduct the volunteer's interview.

Here are some general suggestions for areas you might want to cover in your questionnaire:

- Who recommended the potential volunteer or how they heard about your organization
- Educational background
- Employment history
- Previous volunteering experience
- Clubs or associations they are involved with
- Why they want to volunteer for your organization
- Anything in particular they would like to do for your organization
- Hobbies and other interests

- Available transportation
- Special skills or talents
- Fluency in any language other than English
- Dislikes: What do they do not want to do
- How much time they can volunteer a week
- Whether they would be willing to commit for a year
- If your organization requires one, your questionnaire should provide an opportunity for the prospective volunteer to tell you whether they would agree to a security check

A well-designed questionnaire and interview can also provide clues as to whether the prospective volunteer would fit smoothly into your organization's culture. This is important information, because a frequent reason people give for abandoning their volunteer work is the discord they experienced among volunteers or between staff and volunteers. Your questions and interviews should also try to uncover any indication of hidden agendas or unstable behavior.

There is one other benefit to be derived from the screening questionnaire: the information collected provides invaluable clues about the prospective volunteer that, in the future, can help the volunteer coordinator keep that individual engaged and motivated. With this in mind, you might inquire in your questionnaire if the candidate is connected to any social networking platforms such as Facebook. This information will give the volunteer manager one more way to recognize the volunteer's contribution or show appreciation for his or her help. The manager can acknowledge the volunteer's accomplishments on his or her Facebook wall or whatever space is available on the social networking platform the volunteer uses.

Creating a User-Friendly Record-Keeping System

Before you bring your new volunteers on board, you should have a volunteer record-keeping system in place. This way you can take the information you gathered during recruitment and begin a file on your new volunteer. Whether you keep the information in a file or on the computer, your system should be easy to access. You do not want it tucked away somewhere gathering dust; you want the system to be used.

Your volunteers' information can help you place your volunteers where they will be most effective. You can use it to personalize awards and recognition events and create motivational programs. Nothing helps to keep volunteers involved in an organization more than the feeling they are respected and appreciated, and personalizing your acts of appreciation reinforces that feeling.

However, there is a caveat to this advice: the issue of privacy. Some of your volunteers may be uncomfortable with the idea that information they consider personal — such as addresses, phone numbers, and birth dates — is being made available to strangers. It is essential that you have a policy for the use of this information. Your policy should be in writing, and should assure volunteers that their personal information will only

CHECKLIST FOR VOLUNTEER RECORD KEEPING FILES
☐ Name
☐ Address
☐ Email
☐ Address
☐ Telephone Number
☐ Referred by
☐ Education
☐ Relevant Experience
☐ Skills and Interests
☐ Availability
☐ Starting date
☐ Emergency Contact Information

be used in the context of your volunteer program. The policy should also express access to volunteer information will be limited to employees and supervisory volunteers who have a legitimate need for the information to fill out forms required by law, maintain the organization's records, assign volunteer work, and prepare motivational and reward programs.

Tips for Getting Your Volunteer Recruiting Campaign Off to a Good Start

- Begin by making sure that your recruitment effort is well-focused. Have a plan.

- In designing your recruitment plan, incorporate measurable goals so you can track your success.

- A successful recruitment effort begins with defining your organization's volunteer needs.

- Volunteers require space. Make sure you have the space you need for new volunteers, or a viable plan for sharing staff space that will not negatively affect your staff's productivity.

- "Warm body" recruiting is a philosophy that says all you need to do is have a warm body in place to do what needs to be done. This system is seldom satisfying for the nonprofit or the volunteer. The more specific you can be in targeting volunteers to meet your needs, the better chance you will have of creating a happy, reliable corps of volunteers.

- No one understands where volunteers would be helpful and where they would be a liability better than the staff and volunteers who will be working with them. Consult them.

- Remember who holds the purse strings: Bring your board in early on any planning for a recruitment campaign.

- Compatibility is as important in a volunteer as ability.

- Not just who, but how you recruit will determine the relationship you will have with your prospective volunteers once they become a part of your team.

- It is important to make your organization's needs and expectations clear during the recruiting process. Otherwise you risk disappointing your potential volunteers once they begin working with you.

- Research reveals that two things keeping people from volunteering are the types of work expected of them and a nonprofit's inability to recognize and utilize the potential volunteer's specific skills and talents.

- Volunteer coordinators and recruiters need to be sensitive to the fact that new volunteers will mean added work and increased stress for the staff. Letting your staff know you understand this before you bring new volunteers on board will make for a smoother integration of new volunteers.

- Board members are often well-connected in the community and can be of great help in lining up in-kind and monetary donations for your recruitment campaign. This is another reason to bring them in early in the process.

- A realistic budget is an important part of any recruitment campaign.

- Budgets from previous recruitment campaigns can provide a guideline for a new campaign, but they should be evaluated carefully. Where did the previous campaign go over budget?

What part of the budget gave your organization the "most bang for its bucks?" Is there anything in the previous budget that did not produce the desired results? Do not just replicate the old budget; build a better one from it.

- Take advantage of available free professional help: Enlist qualified board members or volunteers to help you prepare your budget.

- As with any good budget, your recruitment budget should include contingency funds in case an unpredicted opportunity or unexpected expense arises.

- Your volunteer-screening procedure should reflect your organization's risk-management and liability-reduction policies.

- Things happen. Even small, grassroots volunteer organizations need to have a risk-management and liability-reduction plan in place before they begin recruiting volunteers.

- Because a nonprofit organization is responsible for the safety of its employees, volunteers, and clients, it is sound policy to require background checks on all prospective volunteers. This expense should be included in the nonprofit's operational budget under security.

- A user-friendly record-keeping system can be a valuable tool for volunteer coordinators. It can help them place their volunteers where they will be happiest and most effective, and it can enable the volunteer coordinator to personalize his or her efforts to motivate and reward the volunteers.

- While there are similarities between managing employees

and managing volunteers, there is one important difference: Unlike employees, if a volunteer is not comfortable with the people he or she works with, they simply leave. This is an important consideration when your goal is retaining good volunteers.

- The recruitment process presents an opportunity to learn about your potential volunteers' needs and expectations — critical information that helps you ensure their volunteer experience is fulfilling so they will stay and give their best.

- A well-conducted volunteer recruitment campaign wins friends and strengthens a nonprofit's brand by making the recruitment experience pleasant for the candidate. Conversely, a campaign that appears disorganized or unfocused can do irreparable harm to an organization's image.

CHAPTER 2:

PUTTING YOUR HOUSE IN ORDER

The goal of any volunteer program is to attract and keep reliable volunteers, which means creating a comfortable, inviting environment for them. A key factor in accomplishing this is how well your staff relates to your volunteers. To get your staff off on the right foot, you will need to invest some time in preparing them for the influx of new volunteers.

Preparing the Staff for New Volunteers

In the case of a small organization, that preparation could be informal: a matter of some one-on-one conversations or a coffee-hour gathering to discuss the subject. Larger organizations may want to have a meeting, or a series of meetings, with a formal program. Regardless of the form your encounter takes, there are some specific things you will want to cover in these meetings.

First, you want to remind your staff of the value your new volunteers will provide for your organization. Be specific. If they will solve a problem or need, point it out. If they will make a significant contribution to fulfilling your organization's mission or help it meet its financial goals, mention this.

Next, you want to remind your staff of the important role they will be playing in integrating these new volunteers into your organization. They should be made aware of the impact their relationship with these new volunteers will have on your ability to retain them.

There is another very important thing your staff orientation meeting needs to communicate: your understanding that, as valuable as these new volunteers will be, they will also mean more work and, at times, additional stress for your staff.

These discussions should not be one-sided. You need to encourage your staff to express their concerns, and invite them to offer suggestions for all aspect of your recruitment plan. Ask them for ideas on how to effectively integrate the new volunteers. Space needed, scheduling considerations, and other potential problems should be discussed. If you want the integration process to go smoothly, you need to make your staff feel they are true partners in the process. These meetings or conversations also present an opportunity for you to thank your staff for their help.

Talking Points for New Volunteer Orientation Meetings

- Reinforce appreciation of the value of volunteers to your organization.

- Explain the critical role staff members play in your organization's ability to retain volunteers.

- Recognize the additional work and possible pressure the new volunteers will create for your staff.

- Invite staff members to freely discuss their concerns.

- Encourage staff members to offer suggestions or ideas for making the volunteers more comfortable.

- Stress to your staff that they are partners in the process with a stake in its successful outcome.

- Thank them for their help.

While staff-volunteer orientation meetings are designed to smooth the transition of new volunteers into your organization, they offer two valuable bonuses: (1) Taking the time to listen to your staff and respond to their concerns helps build staff morale, and (2) the information and experience your staff shares with you during these meetings increases your understanding of volunteer-staff dynamics. This understanding is a key factor in retaining volunteers.

"A principle learned in the customer service discipline has great relevance when translated to the field of volunteer involvement: 'Staff will tend to treat volunteers in the same way that management treats staff.' Supervisory styles tend to flow."

— **Steve McCurley,** *Building Understanding and Collaboration: Creating Synergistic Relationships Between Staff and Volunteers*

The Case for a Written Staff-Volunteer Relationship Policy

The first thing most nonprofits do is create a mission statement, which is a thoughtfully worded explanation of who they are and what they have formed their organization to accomplish. In the process of staffing their organization, nonprofits usually create job descriptions for their paid staff. They may even print up a handbook for volunteers. But often overlooked is the need for establishing a policy to cover the relationship between their staff and their volunteers.

It is not that a policy does not evolve; it is just that many nonprofit organizations do not take the time to formalize this policy in writing. There are good reasons to make the time. Unwritten policies tend to be understood differently by different people, and they do not carry the weight or hold the authority of a written policy. Therefore, when problems arise, confusion over the policy makes rectifying them more difficult.

In addition to preventing confusion, having a written policy for the relationship between your staff and your volunteers builds understanding and collaboration between these two groups. To this end, it is desirable to have at least one experienced staff member and one experienced volunteer involved in creating the policy.

More important than the details, which will depend on the nature of your organization, is the tone of the document. The wording should clearly reflect the view that paid staff and volunteers are of equal value — that both make an important contribution to the success of the organization's mission. The guidelines should also reflect a respect for the value of both your staff's and your volunteers' time.

Helping Volunteers Understand Their Place in the Organization

There is no tool more powerful in its ability to help turn new recruits into dedicated, long-term volunteers than a well-conceived volunteer handbook. Your handbook should be more than just a collection of information. It should be inviting and easy to read; it should also present a snapshot of your organization that reinforces your volunteer's belief that he or she has made the right decision in becoming a part of your team.

The nature of your organization and your mission will determine what information you need to communicate in the book, but there are certain components that are universal:

- Welcoming message
- Organization's mission statement
- Introduction
- Explanation of organizational structure
- Contact information
- Role of board of directors
- Financial structure of organization
- Volunteers' rights and responsibilities
- What constitutes acceptable and unacceptable behavior
- Description of volunteer training programs
- Confidentiality policies
- Safety and risk-management policies
- Explanation of recognition programs
- Volunteer severance policies

Your welcoming statement will set the tone of your volunteer handbook. It can be from the organization's executive director, the head of the volunteer program, or un-credited. The purpose of the statement is to officially thank the volunteer for choosing your organization to serve and make him or her feel welcome.

Another critical component of your handbook is the introduction. It provides an opportunity for you to tell your story: your organization's history and place in the community, the scope of your services, the geographic area you serve, your affiliations, and your accomplishments and goals. It is especially important because it presents documented proof of your value — information your new volunteers will draw upon repeatedly in their role as your ambassadors to the community.

The nature of the contact information provided will depend on the size and complexity of the organization. The main phone number, street address, and email and website addresses should always be provided. In some organizations a single contact may be listed for all volunteer-related information. A larger organization may provide a variety of numbers depending

on the issue (safety matters may be directed to the safety department, volunteer assignment information may be referred to another number, questions about fund raising another, and event schedules another).

The section on the financial structure of your organization provides another opportunity for you to make your case to the volunteer. Good stewardship is a major factor in a volunteer's selection of which nonprofit to volunteer with. Your presentation of your organization's financial structure should reinforce your image as a good steward. To make your case even stronger, you may want to include a recent annual report with your volunteer handbook.

Careful attention should be paid to the section on volunteers' rights and responsibilities. The handbook should cover, in detail, what the volunteer can expect from your organization in the way of support, as well as what you expect of the volunteer in terms of work and behavior. Training programs should be outlined and your policies on confidentiality and risk management clearly defined.

One last point: As in any partnership, it is valuable to have a procedure for severing the relationship between you and a volunteer. In some states there are even legal implications to dismissing a volunteer. To prevent future problems, this information should be included in your volunteer handbook.

Curtis Hammond, volunteer coordinator for Missoula Aging Services in Western Montana, is a strong believer in the value of having a volunteer handbook, as you can see in his report from the field.

 **VOLUNTEER STORIES FROM THE FIELD**

 **Missoula Aging Services**   337 Stephens Ave.
Missoula, Montana

Website: **www.missoulaagingservices.org**

Missoula Aging Services is an area agency on aging in Western Montana that promotes the independence, dignity, and health of older adults and those who care for them through advocacy, education, services, and volunteer opportunities. They provide services in Missoula County, which has a population of about 107,320 people, and use volunteers in every one of their programs. Those programs include delivering meals, visiting the elderly, and individualized counseling services. The organization's volunteer handbook plays an important role in retaining long-term volunteers and avoiding problems in their volunteer program.

Report from: Curtis Hammond, volunteer coordinator

One of our greatest challenges is finding a way to recruit successfully for difficult programs. We run a program that asks volunteers to assist elders with figuring out their Medicare claims against supplemental insurance and doctor bills, a time consuming and often frustrating procedure. Programs like this that require a lot of training are often difficult to recruit for. Our solution has been to break down the requirements for training, and that seems to have helped. We have not been as successful with another challenge. Many prospective volunteers come to us looking for short-term volunteer opportunities. Unfortunately, because of the nature of our work we don't have many of these to offer. We have no solution for this problem.

Concerning our philosophy about volunteers, we consider them as "non-paid staff." This philosophy has worked very well for us. We have enjoyed a high retention of qualified volunteers and have attracted some very talented volunteers by embracing this ideal. As non-paid staff, our volunteers are invited to staff training sessions, reimbursed for mileage while volunteering, provided with professional courtesy, and are given a higher standing in our agency. Their positions are modeled after paid positions: that is, they are given accurate and individualized job descriptions and a handbook outlining policies and procedures. Because we have a handbook with policies and procedures, we can rely on clearly written guidelines for conduct and grievance procedures. This has been very beneficial to both our paid staff and our volunteers when problems arise.

If your organization has only a small number of volunteers you may feel that you have no need for a volunteer handbook, but before you dismiss the idea, consider this: Regardless of the number of volunteers you have or what they do, your volunteers are perceived by your community as the face of your organization. Their behavior and attitude reflect on your mission. The story they present about your organization may be the only story your community will hear. You may have no need for an elaborate volunteer handbook, but a document that provides a modest recounting of your history and a declaration of your mission, along with some guidelines as to what you expect of your volunteers in the way of performance and behavior, can give you better control over how the public perceives your organization.

For an example of how another volunteer coordinator has turned to the internet and direct contact to keep her widely dispersed team of volunteers informed about policy and procedures, here is a report from the founder and executive director of Alzheimer's Art Quilt Initiative, based in Burton, Michigan.

VOLUNTEER STORIES
FROM THE FIELD

Burton, Michigan

Website: **www.AlzQuilts.org**

The Alzheimer's Art Quilt Initiative is an internet-driven, grassroots, all-volunteer effort to raise awareness of Alzheimer's disease and fund research through art, specifically through quilting. They have an estimated 1,500 volunteer/supporters throughout the United States and overseas who help them turn borrowed and donated quilts into research dollars.

Report from Ami Simms, founder and executive director of Art Quilt Initiative.

Everything we do is done by volunteers: Developing and maintaining our website, quilt photography, processing and uploading pictures, developing exhibits, soliciting prizes, lecturing, processing bids from our silent auctions, the list goes on and on.

All our policies, practices, and information about our organization are on our website. It has been my experience that people do not read directions. Even when they do, most do not retain 100 percent of what they read. When they are stressed they remember even less, and since most of our volunteers are caring for loved ones with this dreaded disease, stress is a major factor with our supporters. We try to give them the information in other ways: through individual emails, in monthly emailed updates, on the phone, in person, with pictures… and *always* with patience and understanding. Their lack of understanding is because of our shortcomings. We are constantly trying to refine our instructions.

Creating a Volunteer Contract

Another way to ensure your volunteers know what is expected of them is to have them sign a contract. This is another item that you should have in place before you bring your volunteers onboard. There are several advantages to having your volunteers sign a contract such as:

- It shows your volunteers that you have respect for the services they are offering.

- It codifies their duties and your responsibilities.

- It clarifies expectations, both yours and theirs.

- It creates a standard by which you can evaluate your volunteer's performance.

- It can be a valuable component in your risk management program, and a safety net in the event that problems arise with that volunteer.

In its simplest form your volunteer contract can merely state the intent of the document and list what your organization agrees to provide for the volunteer and the services you expect in return. You may also want your volunteers to commit to specific training for the position, and include a time frame for the services they will perform.

Organizations in which volunteers interact with clients, or engage in physical activities that present some risk, may want to include information about legal and safety requirements. Nonprofits that offer a variety of volunteer opportunities would be best served by personalized contracts that specify the particular job the volunteer is agreeing to do. If volunteers change positions, you may want to redo the contract to reflect the new position.

Some organizations require only their volunteers to sign the contract, but by adding your signature you are underlining your commitment to the relationship that contract is establishing. If your prospective volunteer is underage, you may want to follow the lead of many nonprofits and require that a parent or guardian co-sign the agreement.

The following sample contract is for guidance only, to help you create a document that reflects the policies and needs of your specific organization.

SAMPLE VOLUNTEER CONTRACT

1. We, (organization's name) accept (volunteer's name) as a valuable member of our volunteer team and welcome his/her agreement to perform the following services for our organization (description of volunteer services to be performed). In light of this volunteer's commitment, we agree to:

    *   Provide the volunteer with a job description detailing his/her duties and responsibilities, as well as any information, training, and support necessary for the performance of this job

    *   Supervise and provide feedback on the volunteer's performance

    *   Respect the volunteer's skills, dignity, and time

    *   Treat the volunteer as an equal partner in the pursuit of our organization's goals and mission

    *   Provide the volunteer with an opportunity for personal growth, professional development, and interaction with other volunteers

2. I (volunteer's name) agree to serve as a volunteer and commit to the following:

    *   To perform my volunteer duties to the best of my abilities

    *   To participate in all required orientation and training sessions

    *   To meet all time and duty commitments, including providing adequate notice any time circumstances prevent me from fulfilling my volunteer obligations

    *   To adhere to all the organization's rules and procedures and maintain the confidentiality of client/agency relations.

3. AGREED TO

    _____   _____
    Volunteer's name   Date

    _____   _____
    Organization's name   Date

    This agreement will expire automatically in ____ months on _____unless renewed by both parties, and may be canceled at any time at the discretion of either party.

Some Tips for Smoothing the Way for New Volunteers

- If you want to ensure a smooth integration of new volunteers into your organization, invest some time in preparing your staff for the influx.

- In making your case to your staff about the need for new volunteers, be specific. Remind them how the new volunteers will ease their workload and help your organization fulfill its mission.

- You do not have to have a meeting to prepare your staff for new volunteers. If you are working with a small group, you can do it one-on-one with casual conversation over a cup of tea, or several brief conversations in the hall.

- Set a celebratory mood for the influx of new volunteers. Instead of holding a meeting, create an event. Gather your staff together with an ice cream social, or solicit their concerns and suggestions after work during an informal get together with hors d'oeuvres and punch or wine.

- Make sure your staff knows you are sensitive to the additional work and possible stress a new batch of volunteers may mean for them.

- During the recruiting process be available to your staff. Make it easy for them to approach you with their concerns and suggestions.

- Put up a special suggestion box for ideas on how to make the new volunteers feel welcome, and reward staff members who come up with innovative ideas.

- Before your new volunteers are brought on board, help your staff brush up on their people skills with a role-playing game.

- Reinforce a positive attitude toward new volunteers by reminding your staff of the positive experiences they have had with your best volunteers. If you are introducing volunteers into your organization for the first time, talk about your former experience with volunteers in other organizations and how helpful they were.

- Focusing on concerns and past problems will reinforce a negative attitude in your staff. Do not ignore your staff's concerns, but balance their feelings by helping them refocus on the advantages the new volunteers will bring to them and to the organization.

- Do not wait until the recruiting process is over to thank your staff for their help. Express your gratitude throughout the process.

- When someone on your staff finds a candidate or a resource for your volunteer effort, recognize their contribution — publicize it within your organization with mention in your newsletter or a note up on the bulletin board.

- Verbal policies are easily misunderstood. If the policy has any value, put it in writing.

- When creating or updating policies for your organization, involve the people who will be affected.

- If you have a space problem hold an agency-wide employee-volunteer contest for creative ideas on how to make the space you have work, and come up with an award for any ideas that you implement. To make the contest more fun, design a lighthearted prize for the wildest idea.

- Ask your staff for suggestions on ways to freshen up the workspace they will be sharing with new volunteers as a welcoming gesture. This will help reinforce the feeling that the new volunteers are going to be a valuable asset for the department and the organization. Involve your staff in implementing the suggestions.

- Invite your staff, board, and current volunteers to make a checklist of what organization publications and information should be included in your volunteer recruitment package.

- Meet with your staff and some of your current volunteers for a constructive conversation about the relationship between the two groups. Arrange for some refreshments to create a comfortable environment. Begin by asking the staff and volunteers to discuss what seems to be working well for both groups. If answers are not forthcoming you can prime the pump by asking the question directly to a volunteer or a staff member. After you have spent some time on what is working segue into a discussion about what situations could be improved. The final portion of the meeting should focus on ideas from all participants on ways to ameliorate any potential areas of conflict. Close the meeting by assuring the group that it has been constructive and thank all participants. Leave the door open for a future meeting to evaluate any changes that were proposed.

- Hold a design contest for creating or improving your employee handbook.

- Ask current volunteers to help you create a volunteer

handbook, or evaluate an existing handbook and offer suggestions for improving it.

- Survey your current volunteers about why they volunteer and why they selected your organization for their services, and use this information in designing your recruitment effort.

- Hold a "think-out-the-box" event for volunteers, board members, and staff to imagine what they would like to see their areas of the organization do or have if money were no object. Then see whether the group can take any of those ideas and pare them down into something workable or come up with an idea to make some of the proposed ideas happen without affecting the organization's financial resources.

- To strengthen the relationship between staff and volunteers before new volunteers are brought on board, ask your volunteers to host a staff-appreciation gathering at one of their homes. It could be a potluck dinner or evening party. Encourage the volunteers to come up with some tangible inexpensive token of their appreciation.

- In determining your volunteer needs do not stop at the obvious. Once you have decided what your immediate needs are, expand your vision. Consider what other talents or skills your organization could use. While those immediate needs should be your primary target, they should not blind you to other possibilities.

- Do not design your recruitment plan in a vacuum. Talk to other volunteer coordinators, check out the volunteer websites on the internet, and thumb through some books on recruiting volunteers for ideas.

CHAPTER 3:

CREATING YOUR RECRUITMENT PACKAGE

With your preliminary work done, now it is time to create your recruiting message. It is not enough just to let people know you are looking for volunteers. You need to give them a reason to want to volunteer for your organization. Having a successful brand is a good place to start. A strong brand reassures potential volunteers that the organization they are considering is reliable and worthy of their services.

What a Brand is and Why You Need One

Almost every day I receive solicitations from nonprofit organizations. Sometimes they try to lure me with heart-tugging pictures or tap into my sense of righteous indignation; sometimes they try guilt. They send me address labels, or even hard cash — a nickel I cannot in good conscience keep, hoping that I will include a check when I return it.

These direct mail pitches do not work with me unless the organization has an established brand that resonates with my concerns. In other words, I need to be presold. That is what a good brand does; it pre-sells the potential donor or prospective volunteer on the value and integrity of the organization so when the "ask" is made, they respond positively.

Bill Nissim, **www.ibranz.com**, a consultant on nonprofit brand management, says that while a nonprofit's brand is its greatest asset, most nonprofits fail to invest the time or money necessary to develop and maintain their brand. This should come as no surprise. A nonprofit's focus is on its mission. The idea of siphoning off any of its precious limited resources for self-promotion goes against the grain.

The problem is that today nonprofits operate in a highly competitive arena, competing for donors and volunteers against an ever-growing number of organizations with equally worthy causes. To succeed in this arena, you need to find a way to stand out in the crowd, a way to communicate to those prospective donors and volunteers that you have the integrity, stewardship, and sense of purpose they are looking for. You need to create an effective brand.

Assessing Your Brand

If your organization has been in operation any length of time, you have a brand. The question is whether your current brand helps or hinders your mission. Do you know how you are being perceived in your community? It does not matter how good a job you are actually doing if the public's perception does not reflect such knowledge, which is why it is critical that a nonprofit stay in tune with how people outside of its organization view it. Here are some suggestions to help you assess your current public image.

- Take an internal survey. Ask your staff, volunteers, and board members how they think the public perceives your organization, based on what they have heard from their families, friends, and neighbors. Chances are most of them have never given this much thought, but how you are perceived in the community has a direct bearing on your organization's ability to carry out its mission. This should not be a one-time exercise. Staying aware of the community's impression of who you are and what you do should be an organization-wide policy. You need to be aware of how you are being perceived so you can constantly fine tune your message to keep your community connection strong.

- Check your press. Most nonprofits keep a file or scrapbook of news stories about their organization. If you have not done this, have a volunteer check the newspapers and TV archives to see how the press has portrayed your organization in the past year. This will give you another snapshot of your current brand.

- Review your organization's logo, stationery, newsletter, and promotional material. Is there a consistency to the image you are presenting with these items? Consistency in the material you put out reflects a sense of professionalism. It is not a matter of spending a large sum of money; it is a matter of planning and coordinating all your outreach materials so they convey to the public that you are organized, focused, and proficient.

- Listen to your community. Hold focus groups. You can hire a professional organization or do this in-house. Ideally, you want to get a cross section of perceptions. One focus group could be made up of business leaders, another of religious leaders, and another of people from various neighborhoods. National organizations should encourage their regional branches to follow this practice. If your organization delivers direct services to your community, you may want to include agencies you work with or clients. Using a variety of focus groups will give you a more complete picture of how your organization is being perceived. Do people have an accurate understanding of your mission? Does your organization enjoy good visibility in the community? Are there any negative perceptions that need to be corrected or positive perceptions that you can build on?

- Compile the information. Have a staff member or volunteer compile all the information you gathered into a report that summarizes the positive and negative aspects of your present image. How close or far from the image you want to project is your community's current perception of you? The answer to this question will tell you what you need to do to shore up or improve your organization's public persona and bring your brand into line with your vision for your organization.

Building a Better Brand

To build a powerful brand first you need to have a clear understanding of your mission and your values. What are you trying to accomplish? Why is what you do important? Who benefits from your work?

TIPS FOR STRENGTHENING YOUR BRAND

- Clarify your mission and values.

- Check your competition.

- Determine what is special about you.

- Understand your community.

- In creating your brand, promise only what you can deliver.

- Create a message that points out your uniqueness and connects with the emotional needs of your community.

- Be consistent. Make sure your brand message is reflected in all your stationary, printed material, advertising, and promotion.

- Maintain awareness of how your organization is viewed in your community to make sure your brand continues to be effective. Tweak when necessary.

Once you have a good sense of who you are, take a hard look at your competition. Is there anything in what you do that sets you apart from other nonprofits in your general field? Is there anything that you do better than anyone else? Can you point out any aspect of what you do that has an intrinsic value that reaches beyond your specific focus to help society in general? Do the services you offer in any way improve the quality of life in your community? Creating a brand is about much more that telling people who you are and what you do. It is about connecting what you do with what is important in *their* lives; it is about creating an emotional bond between you and your prospective donors and volunteers that give them a vested interest in your success.

There are tools that can help: The design of your logo, even the color scheme and the tone of the language you use in your printed material, can infuse an emotional element into your message that can help strengthen your brand. But these are just trappings. It is the message itself that matters most. That message must make a clear case for the value of your work, and do this in terms that address the emotional needs of the people you want to reach. If you fail to make that connection, your brand cannot succeed.

One organization that has done a good job in creating a brand is the Santa Fe Rape Crisis & Trauma Treatment Center in Santa Fe, New Mexico. According to Barbara Goldman, executive director emeritus of SFRC & TTC, there are more than 1,000 not-for-profit organizations operating in Santa Fe, a community with almost no enterprise. The largest employer is the state government — Santa Fe is the state capital — and there is little industry. "When you have that many nonprofits all shaking from the same tree," Goldman says, "believe me, all the plums are gone. It is really hard because the same people, the same merchants are hit upon incessantly." Aside from the competition they face from other nonprofits, SFRC & TTC faces an additional challenge in attracting volunteers because of the sensitive nature of its work.

VOLUNTEER STORIES FROM THE FIELD

Help, Hope and Healing

Santa Fe Rape Crisis & Trauma Treatment Center

Santa Fe, New Mexico

Website: **http://sfrcc.org**

To contact Dr. Goldman: **bgoldman@cybermesa.com**

Report from Barbara Goldman, Ph.D., executive director emeritus

The board members were very insistent that we carefully and thoughtfully brand our organization. We were blessed to have some board members who were excellent at marketing, public relations, and graphics. We started by creating a logo, changing the stationary, changing the name, and we put this new brand on everything that went forward from that time on, no matter what it was. Because we have to stay in the public's consciousness to carry out our mission, we have a multiplicity of events going on all the time. Our brand went everywhere we went.

It wasn't just the graphics and the look. We determined our message. Rape, particularly when you are dealing with children, and the other traumas we deal with — they are hard to hear about. When I went out to speak, I really had to make sure that I didn't leave people shell shocked … that I made them understand that we were not about the violence, but about bring help, hope, and healing.

Because 80 percent of the people a rape crisis center deals with are women, you have to be very careful that people understand that this just doesn't happen to women — it's not a feminist issue; it is a human issue. You will lose volunteers, you will lose donors, you will lose everything if you do not communicate the big picture of who you serve. There are plenty of little boys and men who have been sexually violated who, because of the way we socialize our children, will never come forward. You always have to remember that whatever cause you work with, you've got to make the mission be more expansive than the mythology.

There is another critical key to creating a successful brand. Nonprofits tend to have a vision that extends beyond their current ability. This optimism fuels their growth. Creating a successful brand, however, requires a more pragmatic approach. Your brand is a promise you make to the community and it tells them what they can expect of you. If you build your brand around what you would like to do, instead of what you are currently capable of doing, you are bound to disappoint. Failing to fulfill the promise your brand makes will destroy your credibility.

A strong brand is not built overnight. It takes time, diligence, insight, and imagination. Once you have created a brand that is true to your vision for your organization, you need to make a commitment to maintain and protect this valuable asset. You also need to periodically check to see whether your brand is still resonating with your community, and tweak your message whenever you sense it may be losing its power.

Using Your Brand to Build Your Recruiting Message

If you have a strong brand, you are ahead of the game when you go to put your recruitment package together. You already have a well-crafted history of your organization and other coordinated promotional materials that can be included in your recruitment package, or used as a resource to create new, specifically focused handouts for your package.

If you do not have a strong brand, your recruitment effort is a good place to begin building one. You can start by creating a new history document that projects a compelling image of your organization; one that helps people see it as you want it to be seen.

Because you want your recruitment package to look purposeful and professional, not something just thrown together, all the other material you include should reflect the style and design of this new document. Having an integrated look for your recruitment package may seem like a small thing, but it conveys a subtle message that is important to your prospective volunteers. The planned, organized look of your recruitment package reassures them that you are a solid, capable, professional organization able to put their time and talents to good use.

Your recruitment activities offer you an ideal opportunity to carry this new vision of your organization out into the community, thereby laying the groundwork for your new, more powerful brand.

In putting together your recruitment package, here are a few things to keep in mind:

- You want to tell your organization's story simply and clearly in a manner that makes an emotional connection with your audience. One way to do this is to spotlight your volunteer program, and stress the vital role volunteers play in the important work you do.

- Have someone not connected with putting the package together check to make sure what has been written is clear and easily understood.

- Your recruitment package should spell out your specific needs. There are two reasons for this: (1) Understanding what you are looking for helps your prospective volunteers see how they can fit into your organization. (2) Providing this information enables you to turn your prospective volunteers into recruiters by asking them to relay your needs to their family, friends, and co-workers.

- Your recruitment package should include accurate contact information, preferably the name and telephone number of an individual who can talk the candidate through the process of becoming a volunteer.

We will discuss the use of email and your website for recruiting new volunteers in Chapter 5, but even if you use these tools for recruitment, the last point above is still valid. There is nothing more welcoming to a prospective volunteer than a friendly voice that can answer questions and thank them for their interest in your organization. This kind of personalized response sends an important message. It tells the prospective volunteer that he or she will be respected and appreciated, and that someone will be there to support them through the process of volunteering. If using your website is your only option for receiving volunteer applications, consider assigning someone to make a follow-up call to give the process a more personal touch.

There is another way you can show your respect for your future volunteers' time. List a specific time schedule for contacting your new volunteer coordinator, and make sure someone is available to talk to the prospective volunteers who call at those times. There is nothing more frustrating for someone who is ready to make a commitment than having to waste time leaving messages and waiting for someone to call them back.

What to Look for in a Volunteer

There are special traits that seem to make a person a better volunteer. Consider the experiences of Halle Tecco, the founder of Yoga Bear, a 501(c)3 nonprofit dedicated to providing cancer survivors with more opportunities for wellness and healing through the practice of yoga.

VOLUNTEER STORIES
FROM THE FIELD

Yoga Bear
San Francisco, California
Website: **www.yogabear.org**

Yoga Bear is one of a growing number of online volunteer organizations that are changing the face of volunteerism in the United States. By partnering with more than 135 yoga studios across the Country, Yoga Bear is able to match cancer survivors with free yoga classes in their community. All this is done with a team of 30 volunteers who keep the organization going and growing. Yoga Bear divides the area they cover into regions. Each region has a chapter director who supervises volunteer managers. These managers work at building relationships with studios and being a "buddy" to the cancer survivors enrolled in the program. Yoga Bear's volunteer social media coordinator updates the organization's Facebook and Twitter accounts. Yoga Bear also has volunteer grant writers, public relations experts, web designers, and yoga instructors.

Report from Halle Tecco, founder, Yoga Bear

Everything we have accomplished has been done on the backs of unpaid volunteers. We have perhaps two or three people doing what would be one full-time, paid staff job. In the beginning, we took any volunteer who wanted to get involved. We had no choice. We were a new nonprofit without the resources or track record to attract a large volume of high-caliber volunteers. But after we built up our brand, volunteers began flocking to our organization, and we were able to filter.

I studied the characteristics of our highest contributing volunteers and found a few common traits that worked really well in our organization. These included boldness and confidence, attention to detail, and self-motivation. So as I filtered and interviewed potential volunteers, I became more selective and gave preference to true leaders with those qualities. The long-term results have been dramatic. Our retention rate is up, and these volunteers have followed through with their commitment and beyond.

After their initial training, Halle Tecco's volunteers work independently in their communities, so it is understandable that the four qualities she looks for in a volunteer are boldness, confidence, attention to detail, and self-motivation.

Lawrence Becerra, who coordinates volunteers for Las Campanas Compadres in Sante Fe, New Mexico, has a different set of criteria. His organization provides individuals who have physical, emotional, or learning disabilities with an opportunity for therapeutic physical skill development. The organization uses volunteers to assist the professional teachers on the staff. Because these volunteers work directly with the organization's clients, Becerra looks for traits like compassion, patience, and sensitivity when recruiting volunteers.

Woody Carlson, the minister of the Wooden Cross Lutheran Church in Woodinville, Washington, coordinates volunteers for the local Habitat for Humanity program. The houses constructed under this program are built primarily by unskilled volunteer help. Most technical assistance and materials are donated, which makes for an erratic construction schedule. Because of the unpredictable "hurry up and wait" nature of the work schedule, volunteers often spend a great deal of time sitting around and waiting for people or materials to show up. This is why the trait Carlson appreciates most in his volunteers is flexibility. A sense of humor, he says, also helps.

When you begin looking for new volunteers, you too will search out people with traits that suit them for the work you need them to do. Here is another guideline to help you find the best volunteers for your organization. According to most of the volunteer coordinators contacted for this book, their best volunteers share some or all of the following ten traits:

- An ability to get along with people
- A cheerful disposition
- Patience
- Self-motivation
- Flexibility
- Organizational skills
- Dedication
- Reliability
- Attention to details
- A sense of humor

Understanding what traits successful volunteers share is particularly valuable during the recruiting process because if you know the kind of person you are looking for, you can target your recruitment message for that type of individual. When designing the questions for your screening process, it enables you to create questions that expose the presence or absence of some of these traits in your prospective volunteers. For example, you might ask the candidate to tell you about an experience he or she has had at work or personally that tested their patience, or gave them particular pleasure or satisfaction. You might ask them to explain how, in the past, they handled a complex assignment or what they have done to get themselves going on a project they did not want to do. Questions about the candidate's family can give you clues to their ability to deal with interpersonal relationships, and questions about their job can give you clues about how they deal with people. Chapter 6 addresses this in further detail. Beyond the recruiting process, knowing what makes a good volunteer can help volunteer trainers and coordinators cultivate and encourage these positive traits in their volunteers through example and by recognizing and rewarding them.

What About Age

Have you given thought to age in drawing up your volunteer profile? What an AARP study has dubbed "The Experienced Generation" — Americans between the ages of 44 and 79 — seems to be the most sought-after demographic for volunteering in this country, but young people are also a valuable resource for nonprofits. Students can bring a special kind of energy to an organization. They can provide a fresh perspective, and thanks to their computer savvy, they can often provide needed technical skills, as evidenced by this next volunteer story from the field.

VOLUNTEER STORIES
FROM THE FIELD

Link to Libraries Inc.
East Longmeadow, Massachusetts
Website: **www.linktolibraries.org**

Link to Libraries Inc. is a not-for-profit organization whose mission is to collect and distribute new and gently used books to public elementary schools and nonprofit organizations in Western Massachusetts and Northern Connecticut. They are also committed to enhancing the language and literacy skills of children from all cultural backgrounds to enable them to learn about their world through reading. Link to Libraries Inc. operates with a board and volunteer staff of 12 who serve approximately 3,000 youths a year. Volunteers assist with fundraising program development, make presentations, deliver books to schools, attend to office work, and are involved in community outreach. Volunteers were also responsible for the development of the organization's website, which was launched in June of 2009.

Report from Susan Jaye-Kaplan, president and founder, Link to Libraries Inc.

It is our philosophy at Link to Libraries that volunteers, regardless of their age, should be treated with dignity and great respect. We work hard to make our volunteers feel vested in our program, and to let them know they are appreciated.

We have an eighth-grade volunteer, a 14-year-old boy, who wanted to develop our website. We decided to let this young man run with his idea. He went to work and, with the help of an adult mentor and input from family and friends, completed the job. Not only did he enable us to get our website developed, but his accomplishment served to motivate other teens to get involved with our organization. Watching him, they came to understand their views and ideas were meaningful to us, and would be honored. As a result of this philosophy, the greatest challenge I have is keeping volunteers from being over-worked and having them take more on than they can do out of their excitement and their commitment to the Links to Libraries programs. But this is a good thing.

High school and college students volunteer for many reasons, including:

- To build their résumés
- To feel like they are contributing something to their community
- To try out a skill or sample a career possibility
- To meet volunteering requirements of their school, fraternity, or sorority

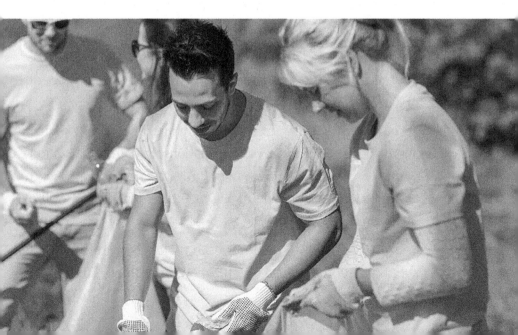

If you are interested in recruiting students, your best source would be the schools in your area. Even if they do not have a formal program for placing their students in volunteer positions, they will usually be happy to relay your need for volunteers to their students.

Some Tips for Creating an Effective Volunteer Recruitment Package

- Intended or not, your organization has a brand. Good or bad, weak or strong, that brand affects how your organization is perceived, and how effective you are in fulfilling your mission. Pay attention to it, and make sure it is conveying the message you intend to convey.

- Having a powerful brand is important for nonprofits because an effective brand pre-sells potential donors and prospective volunteers on an organization's value and integrity, so they will react positively to requests for donations or invitations to become volunteers.

- If you want to protect your brand — your public persona — make it organizational policy to periodically check how you are being perceived in your community. If you sense your brand is weakening, take immediate steps to revitalize it.

- A volunteer recruitment campaign presents an excellent opportunity to boost your image in the community. Think of your recruiters as goodwill ambassadors, and your recruitment materials as part of a public relations campaign.

- To be effective your recruitment campaign should not be just about you. It should be about the relationship your organization wants to create with its new volunteers and the value you and those volunteers will create together for the good of the community.

- Your logo, letterhead, and outreach materials speak volumes about who you are as an organization. Coordinated in design, they suggest a capable, professional organization in control of its mission. Erratically produced with no sense of unity, they suggest disorganization and lack of focus.

- Creating a professional, integrated look for your organization does not necessarily require spending much money. It does, however, require that everyone focuses on maintaining a unified look for all outreach materials. One way to do this is to have one person check all outreach material as it is being designed. Another way is to have a basic format for use of your logo and for your color scheme.

- Redesigning on the cheap: If you want a new look for your logo, stationery, and outreach materials, but do not have a budget for the project, mine the hidden talent in your organization. Hold a design contest for staff and volunteers. Encourage ideas as well as renderings. If you find a design that works, see whether anyone on your board or any of your volunteers can arrange for a local printing company to donate all or part of the cost of developing the design in return for getting the printing job.

- If positive stories about your organization or your work have been printed, get tear sheets or make copies of them to include in your recruitment package.

- Local and neighborhood newspapers can be advocates for your organization during recruiting efforts. To maintain a good relationship, send personalized thank-you notes when they help you out, print a positive story about your work, mention you in a positive light in a major story, or even print a positive letter from a reader in their letters to the editor section. Building goodwill is a continuous process.

- Take time to analyze the character traits of your best volunteers. Use this information in screening for new volunteers.

- While traits like patience, reliability, and organizational skills are usually ingrained in a person, they can be cultivated in an individual in whom they do not naturally occur. By reinforcing the value of these traits and encouraging them through acknowledgement and reward, you can help your volunteers develop them. Before you launch your recruitment campaign, get to know your community, and give them a chance to get to know you. Hold an open house for community leaders or the general public. Give the event added value by honoring someone in the community who has helped your organization. Prepare a brief program to explain who you are and what you do. Invite the local press, including reporters from neighborhood publications. Do not wait for your guests to ask questions; be prepared to ask them about their perceptions of you, and their opinions about the work you do.

- Handling negative feedback about your organization is always a challenge. Nothing is accomplished by becoming defensive. It is better to accept the criticism graciously, thank the party making it, and assure them that you will try to rectify the situation if you can. If you are able to do something to defuse the complaint, follow up by letting the individual know. If the criticism is unwarranted, just letting the individual know you are paying attention to the complaint usually squelches the problem.

- Do some pre-recruiting intelligence work. Hold a "bring-a-friend" evening — a small party for your staff, volunteers, and some of their friends. Use the opportunity to test your recruitment package. Solicit feedback from your guests on the material: Is it clear? Do they understand what your organization is about — what you do? Do they understand what the volunteers you recruit will be doing? Use the feedback to refine your package.

- To make sure everyone in your organization understands your mission, try this exercise. Print out copies of your mission statement and pass them out to everyone involved with your organization. Ask them to review the mission statement and write a paragraph about what they think it means and how well your organization is fulfilling this mission. Instruct them not to consult each other before completing the assignment. Collect the completed papers and in an organization-wide meeting have them read aloud. Open the meeting up for discussion after each paper is read. Read enough of these submissions to get a conversation going about what your mission statement means, and how well your organization is meeting its commitment. Direct the conversation toward a consensus of what the statement means, and an evaluation of how well it is being met. If there are areas where the organization is falling short, invite suggestions for ways to rectify this weakness.

- Hold an in-house event to launch your recruitment outreach. Thank the people who have gotten everything in place. Bring everyone else up to date on how the campaign will unfold. Be receptive to suggestions or offers of help, incorporating those suggestions that would be helpful into your plans.

- Smaller organizations seldom have clearly defined recruiting efforts. Recruiting for them is usually an ongoing process, which makes maintaining an effective brand even more important. If your area of service is limited, maintaining visibility in your community can be a major challenge. To strengthen your visibility, thoroughly indoctrinate your volunteers in your mission, how well you are fulfilling it, and what your work means to the community. Then send them out into the community to talk about your work — at their place of worship, their children's school, and at any civic organization they belong to. Make being a goodwill ambassador for your organization a part of your volunteer's job description. There is no better recruiting tool than a happy volunteer.

- If being a good steward is one of your strong points as an organization, consider including a telescoped version of your annual report or a statement about how you use your finances in your recruitment package. Stewardship is a major consideration for many people who decide to volunteer for a nonprofit organization.

- To give your recruitment package a competitive edge, include some brief testimonials with pictures from some happy volunteers.

- If you perform direct services to the community, including a few testimonials from your clients in your recruitment package adds credibility to your work.

- Timing is everything. To ensure the success of your volunteer recruitment outreach make sure you roll out your campaign in a timely manner. Summer is not a good time to try to recruit people with school-age children. If you live in an area with harsh winter weather, winter is not a good time to try to recruit older people. If you are looking for college students, the beginning of a semester enables you to use the university's communication channels to reach your prospective volunteers. Launching a recruitment campaign at a time when there are many events scheduled in the community will make it more difficult for you to get press space or in-kind donations from businesses that have probably been hit by many other charities.

- When recruiting volunteers, be aware of your competition — organizations with a similar mission or organizations that attract the same kind of people you are looking for. If you can, find a reason your potential volunteers would be happier volunteering with you, and present this information in your recruitment package.

- One picture is worth 1,000 words. If you provide a direct service to the community, consider including pictures of your activities in your recruitment package.

CHAPTER 4:

LAUNCHING YOUR RECRUITMENT CAMPAIGN

There is a tendency to be nostalgic when we think about how easy it was to find volunteers back in the days when nonprofits could count on a ready pool of stay-at-home mothers eager for a brief reprieve from their daily routines. The truth is, thanks to ever-improving technology, recruiting volunteers is easier and more efficient today. While handing out flyers and posting them in public places is still a viable avenue for getting your recruitment message out, there are now many more efficient ways to get the job done. But before we explore the new technological advances in recruiting, here are some tips on how to get the most out of some old-fashioned, tried-and-true methods.

Word-of-Mouth Recruiting

The least expensive, most effective recruiting tool you have is word-of-mouth (WOM) recruiting. It has become so important in marketing that there are now marketing agencies that specialize in it. Brad Fay is co-founder of one of those agencies, the Keller Fay Group. Speaking at an American Marketing Association conference for nonprofits on July 2, 2006, he pointed out that more than 50 percent of Americans report they are highly likely to trust recommendations from friends and family and pass them on. In other words, people tend to trust information delivered word-of-mouth from credible sources. The question here is not whether WOM is valuable, but what is the most effective way to use it for recruiting volunteers.

Ambassadors who can help you get out your recruitment message:

1. **Volunteers**

2. **Board Members**

3. **Office Staff**

4. **Counselors & Therapists**

The place to start is with your current volunteers. There is no more effective recruiter for a nonprofit than a happy volunteer. Their experience gives them unimpeachable credibility and their enthusiasm encourages confidence in your organization. Volunteer board members, in particular, make excellent ambassadors as their position provides them with an overview of your organization, its vision, and its needs and accomplishments.

Aside from your volunteers, you have some other possible candidates for your recruiting effort. Nonprofits tend to attract employees with a vested interest in their mission. If you have this type of employee, you might want to give them an opportunity to join your WOM outreach team.

Nonprofits that provide services to the community — such as a rape crisis center, a homeless shelter, or a cancer support organization — often have professional therapists or counselors on their staff. Paid or volunteer, these individuals can provide credible testimony about the good you are accomplishing in the community. While client confidentiality needs be respected, by speaking of their work in general terms or sharing stories without revealing names, they can make your mission real and meaningful for potential volunteers, and should be encouraged to help with your recruiting WOM outreach.

Before you send people out on a recruitment mission, it is a good idea to make sure they have all their facts straight and that they fully understand the kind of brand you are trying to build or protect. You can accomplish this by providing some form of standardized training for your outreach volunteers. The more they understand your mission  and what you hope to accomplish with this recruitment program, the better ambassadors they will be for your organization.

There is, of course, the traditional person-to-person WOM approach — one friend telling another. Ideally, that is something that goes on all the time with your organization. What this book will explore is a more organized, targeted type of WOM campaign: one in which the ambassadors you send out spread the word one *group* at a time.

> "Every meeting, every encounter, and every conversation is another opportunity to tell your organization's story."
> — **Barbara Goldman, Ph.D.,** *executive director emeritus, Santa Fe Rape Crisis & Trauma Treatment Center*

How to Use Your Word-Of-Mouth Ambassadors

To attract volunteers, especially quality volunteers, you need to create a buzz. You want to raise your organization's visibility in the community. If people do not know who you are and what you do, why would they want to offer you their services? To do this you need to get your story out, and the first step is to find a venue in which to tell it.

You could hold an open house or hire a hall. Both are viable solutions, but both involve an expenditure of precious financial resources. And you would have to create some kind of event that would make people want to come. A better and less expensive idea is to arrange for your ambassadors to meet the public on their home turf. Places of worship, civic and social organizations, and business groups — even corporations — offer this opportunity. They all have meetings with agendas that include a speaker.

Taking advantage of this opportunity requires some pre-planning. These meetings are usually programmed in advance. If you want to get on the schedule you need to contact the organizations at the beginning of their operational year. If you miss that deadline, your other option is to offer to fill in when a previously scheduled speaker is not able to make it, which requires flexibility. You will need to keep two or three people on call who you can mobilize at any moment.

A word of caution: You will discover that some of your presenters will be better than others, and there will be a temptation to over-use them. This creates two problems: There is a good probability that by overworking your more skilled presenters you will burn them out and end up losing them. And by under-using your less skilled presenters, you will probably see their enthusiasm wane, and you will end up losing them too. A possible way to prevent this loss is to create speaking teams, pairing a skilled presenter with a less-skilled presenter. As the less- skilled presenter gains experience and confidence, you can move them up to the lead speaker position.

Finding Your Speaking Venues

If you have ever been responsible for putting a program together for a meeting, you know that people who coordinate these programs will usually welcome an offer to provide a speaker. However, when seeking a speaking engagement for your organization, it does not hurt to invest in a little insurance.

 One way to improve your odds of being put on the agenda is if your speaker or the person making the request is affiliated with the congregation or association. Another way is to make a connection between your mission and an area the organization is interested in. For example, if the religious organization has been involved in feeding the poor and your mission relates to this, they would be interested in hearing about your work. If the civic organization or the corporation has a history of trying to solve the problem of the homeless and this is an area you work in, you could use this interest to make your connection. Or you might want to appeal to their desire to be good citizens or their concern for the community.

As with any marketing effort — and that is what recruiting for volunteers is — you need to shape your message so it addresses some aspect of your targeted audience's needs or interests.

Meeting venues provide an excellent environment for recruiting, and some ancillary advantages:

- They permit you to meet your potential volunteers in an environment they already trust, which increases their trust in you.

- While you are there to recruit volunteers, these more intimate venues provide you with a valuable opportunity to strengthen your brand. One of the most important things you want to do in telling your story is to make it meaningful to the people who are hearing it. It is easier to make that emotional connection when your audience shares a common interest or common values. Knowing what they care about allows you to point out the aspects of your mission that relate to those concerns, something that is not always possible when you are talking to a diverse audience or trying to get your story across on a printed page.

- These more intimate venues provide an opportunity for interaction: a chance for you to learn how you are being perceived, correct misconceptions, and reinforce positive perceptions.

- If in your recruitment material you also include an opportunity for your audience to donate, you will give those not interested or unable to volunteer an alternative way to act upon the enthusiasm you have generated for your organization.

Bringing the Recruiting Campaign Home

A concept pioneered by World Vision to reach out to sponsors provides us with another possible venue for getting out the word on your volunteer needs: volunteer-hosted dinner parties. One of your current volunteers hosts a dinner party, or even a luncheon, for a handful of friends to introduce them to the gratifying experience of volunteering for your organization. The congeniality of the location and the credibility of the enthusiastic volunteer-host add power to your recruitment message.

In this arrangement, the volunteer provides the food and guests and your organization provides the recruitment information. Blow-ups of pictures showing your volunteers in action or your organization at work can be used for decorations. If you have a video of some aspect of your work, this should be included as part of the program. You could also supply a speaker for the event — perhaps the executive director, or a therapist or a counselor who works with your clients. Another possibility is a volunteer who has a talent for entertaining and can illustrate the fun side of volunteering.

Never lose sight of the fact that most volunteers expect their volunteering experience to be fun. Find a way to project the fun aspect of being a volunteer into all of your presentations.

To come up with some ideas of your own, think about your organization, your volunteers, and your community, then play the "what if" game. What if you offered to send a speaker to a local corporation that has been supportive of your work to talk about your volunteer program? What about a local college that encourages students to provide services to the community? Is there a restaurant that has worked with you that might be open to hosting a recruitment event?

A variation of this idea worked well for a community orchestra that combined recruitment and fundraising in a single event. The orchestra provided the music; the restaurant provided the venue and a limited amount of food; and the guests purchased drinks and more food. After the event, the restaurant owner donated a percentage of the profits from the evening to the orchestra, and the orchestra signed up a number of new volunteers.

If you think it is time to breathe some new life into your volunteer program, then it is time to begin thinking of creative new ways to get your story out.

Working with Local Media

While WOM proponent Brad Fay stresses the importance of word-of-mouth marketing, he does not suggest it as a replacement for the use of media but instead sees the two as inter-related. According to Fay, nearly 40 percent of WOM suggestions are prompted by a newspaper article, a television or radio show, or some form of advertising.

Purchasing an ad promoting your campaign is an obvious way to use media. However, if you are a small nonprofit, you probably do not have financial resources to squander, so let us concentrate on ways to gain this media exposure without having to pay. Your first assignment is to familiarize yourself with the media outlets in your community. There is probably at least one daily newspaper. There are also probably a number of neighborhood publications that are printed weekly or monthly. What about radio stations? Do you have one that is locally owned? These are becoming harder to find as large media conglomerates continue to buy up local stations in town after town. However, even some of these corporate-controlled stations maintain a calendar format that allows local organizations to submit event-oriented announcements.

Local television stations are usually more conscientious in helping to promote nonprofit activities, particularly if they have a regular program that spotlights community interests and events. And you probably have a public radio and a public television station in town or close by. These are frequently affiliated with a university or community college.

Once you have compiled your local media list, put a volunteer to work finding out who in each of these organizations would be your best contact. What reporters at the daily newspaper cover nonprofit activities? Do the television and radio stations have programs that focus on community events, or are there other staff members who write about your area of service? For example, if you work with the homeless, check whether a reporter has shown an interest in this issue. If you are involved with medical research, have you noticed any consistency to the bylines that have appeared on this issue?

Do not overlook those neighborhood weeklies or the free publications found in many communities. Because you will not be competing with hard news for space, you will have a chance for greater exposure. These publications do not have as broad a readership as daily newspapers, but they have a more focused one. People read these papers specifically to find out what is going on in their community, and they usually read the entire publication from front to back.

In most communities, public television and public radio stations have some form of local programming designed to highlight community events and organizations. Public radio stations frequently have local personalities with drive-time shows or someone who inserts news of community interest into their nationally generated news and public-interest programming. Locally produced programs like these are often open to featuring local organizations with something timely and of community interest going on.

Do your homework. Familiarize yourself with the media dynamics in your community. Pay attention to community-focused feature articles in local publications. Watch your local

TV news. Some cable companies provide local programming that focuses on the community. See whether there is anything in your story that would fit into this niche.

Make contacts. Get to know people at the daily and weekly newspapers and the television and radio stations. Indoctrinate them in your story. Get someone from the local media on your board. When the time comes to reach out for volunteers, you will have these resources in place.

To help you stay focused and organized as you gather your information, compile a media file and create a contact sheet to keep track of whom you have contacted, when you made the contact, and the results. This is especially important if more than one person is working on contacting the media. Below is a sample media contact sheet that you can adapt or expand upon to meet your specific needs.

MEDIA CONTACT SHEET						
ORGANIZATION	ADDRESS	CONTACT	TELEPHONE NUMBER	DATE OF CONTACT	FOCUS OF PITCH	OUTCOME
DAILY NEWSPAPER						
NEIGHBORHOOD WEEKLY						
TV STATION						
TV STATION						
TV STATION						
LOCAL RADIO STATION						
PUBLIC TELEVISION STATION						
PUBLIC RADIO STATION						
OTHER						
OTHER						

Creating a Press Release

The media will play a major role in getting news to the community about your recruitment campaign. Before you contact a newspaper or any other media outlet, however, you are going to need to create a press release. This is true even if you are fortunate enough to have a contact at the newspaper or radio or television station.

The purpose of a press release is to encourage reporters or editors at a newspaper or media outlet to create news stories and features based on the information about your recruitment efforts that you have provided. To be effective, your information must be perceived as newsworthy, or at least of interest to their readers, listeners, or viewers. If you are an organization with a good brand and an established presence in the community, your campaign will most likely be seen as newsworthy. If you are not well established, you need to use your press release to make a case for the value of the information to the community.

Timing will also affect how, or even if, your material will be used. Send it too far in advance of your event and it will be put aside, and will likely get lost in the pile. Send it too close to the event, and the reporter or editor will not have enough lead time to do anything with it. Lead time varies from publication to publication and station to station. As you research your media outlets, be sure to find out what their lead time for a press release is.

In preparing your press release there are certain rules and taboos you need to be aware of:

- You should limit your headline to one sentence, and it should tell what your press release is about. Be creative, but not at the cost of clarity or accuracy.

- Capitalize the first letters of all the words in your headline — not all the letters.

- Do not use an exclamation mark in your headline. You are reporting, not commenting.

- Write your release in third person. Think of it as a report being presented by a neutral observer.

- The body of your copy should be no more than two paragraphs or approximately 500 words.

- The first sentence should connect with the readers and pique their curiosity. Again, you can be creative, but keep the copy clear and to the point.

- The first paragraph should give all the critical information so if the readers read no further they will know everything they need to know. Be sure to include the five W's the editor is going to look for: Who, What, When, Where, and Why.

- Use the second paragraph to provide details. Is there anything special about your campaign? Are any celebrities or local personalities involved? Are you holding any special events in relationship to your recruitment effort? Are any local businesses or other organizations partnering with you in your effort? Is there any sense of urgency? Is there any historic value to your campaign or the work you do that you would like to remind people about? In general, is there anything about your campaign and the way you are carrying it out that could be perceived as newsworthy?

- And finally — of critical importance — include sufficient, accurate contact information. The quickest way to ensure you will *not* get media coverage is to fail to give the media outlet a reliable contact number for checking information or finding out more about the event or issue covered in your press release.

You can use your organization's letterhead or, given the versatility of today's word processing programs, you may want to create a form specifically for your press releases. The following sample will provide a guide for formatting the text:

[INSERT ORGANIZATION'S LOGO HERE]

Contact: Mary Jones, Media Coordinator   FOR IMMEDIATE
Telephone: 555-123-4567   RELEASE
Cell phone   555-123-5465
Fax   555 -123-5557
Email: mjones@thisorganization.com
Name of contact here

Title of Your Press Release Here

Begin the first paragraph of your release here. Write in third person reporting style. Your first sentence should capture the reader's interest and make them want to read further. Keep your language direct and clear. Include all pertinent information so the reader will know everything they need to know if they read no more than this first paragraph. Be sure to include the five W's of a good journalistic lead: Who, Why, When, What, and Where.

Begin your second paragraph here. This is where you can expand on the facts presented in the first paragraph. A quote from an official in your organization would be used here, and any facts or arguments you can make that your recruitment effort is newsworthy. Fill in the details about the campaign. Maintain your reporting style. Do not embellish. Do not make any suggestions for how the material should be used, but provide enough information to lead the editors to believe that your event or issue will be of interest or value to their readers, listeners, or viewers. If you need a third paragraph to present all the information, write one, but try not to go over 500 words for the release. What you are aiming for is a quick read that, in as few words as possible, states your case.

For more information, please contact Mary Jones at 555 123 4567or email her at

mjones@thisorganization.com

Your press release is a news-related document, not a promotional piece. It should contain no fluff or hype, just the facts. Respect that the recipients know how to do their job; never tell them how to use the material you send them.

Your press release can be used for more than informing your local media about your recruitment effort. There are other organizations that might be interested to learn about your need for volunteers.

Most public utilities and private corporations use in-house publications to communicate with their employees. Some produce newsletters to send out with their bills. The editors of these publications frequently include community-focused news of interest to their employees or customers. You can expand your outreach by putting these editors on your press release mailing list.

How to Get More Mileage out of a Press Release

You can also use a press release to generate a story about your organization that not only informs the community about your need for volunteers, but also reinforces your organization's brand. Here are a few ideas to get your creative juices flowing.

- Honor a local business or organization that has supported your volunteer program with   services or sponsorship. Time the occasion immediately before or to coincide with the launching of your recruitment campaign. Send out a press release on the newsworthy event stressing the volunteer connection. Include information about your upcoming or current recruitment campaign and contact information prospective volunteers can use.

- If you are a service organization, do you have a success story about one of your clients that involves a volunteer? Honor that volunteer and put out a press release giving the reason the volunteer is being honored. Again, time the release to immediately precede or coincide with the launching of your recruitment outreach and include contact information for anyone wishing to volunteer. A press release like this might prompt a newspaper or media outlet to contact you for a feature story.

- Appoint some volunteer leaders for your recruitment campaign. Find out what weekly neighborhood paper is distributed where each of them lives. Send these papers a news release about the appointment of the volunteer from their circulation area, and tell them that the volunteer is available for an interview. Include information about your volunteer outreach including a contact number for anyone interested in volunteering.

These are just a few ideas to get you thinking about the possibilities in your community. With a little brainstorming with your volunteers and staff you will likely come up with many more as you maneuver through all the details of launching your volunteer recruitment campaign.

Some Tips for Getting Your Recruitment Message Out

- For nonprofits large and small, word-of-mouth marketing is the least costly, most effective way to communicate your need for volunteers to your community.

- Word-of-mouth does not just mean person to person. It can also mean person to group.

- Your best ambassador for carrying your recruitment message into the community is a happy volunteer.

- Board members make effective volunteer recruitment ambassadors because their position gives them an overview of your organization, its vision, its work, and mission.

- Therapists or counselors who work with a nonprofit's clients can be credible witnesses to the organization's value to the community and should be given the opportunity be a part of your volunteer recruitment program. While client confidentially must be protected, by relating stories of their successes without revealing identifying details, these professionals can make the agency's work meaningful for prospective volunteers.

- Places of worship and social and civic organizations can provide effective venues for telling the community about your need for volunteers.

- In the course of explaining your recruitment needs to congregations and organizations you will help these groups learn more about your mission and your work, and this will strengthen your brand in the community.

- If you include information on how to donate in your recruitment package, individuals who do not want to, or cannot, volunteer will have another way to act on the goodwill generated by your recruitment ambassadors.

- With many people involved in getting your message out, maintaining consistency can be a challenge. One solution is to have a standardized training program for all volunteers who will be speaking on behalf of your organization during your volunteer recruitment outreach. This will help ensure your recruitment ambassadors understand your mission, the brand your organization is trying to build or protect, and the specific message you want delivered to prospective volunteers.

- If you want your press release to be considered for publication or trigger an interview on radio or television, timing is crucial. Send it too early and you risk having it put aside and possibly lost. Send it too late — too close to the event — and the editor will not have sufficient lead time to do anything with it. Check the publication or media outlet for their guidelines for submissions.

- A major mistake some nonprofits make is confusing a press release with a publicity release. A press release is a news-related document. It is designed to alert editors and media to a possible news or feature story that might be of interest to their audience. This is why it is written in third person. It should contain no hype or promotion, just the facts.

- It does not matter how newsworthy your press release is, if you do not provide valid, reliable contact information so the editor can check facts and obtain additional information, it will end up in the waste basket.

- To broaden your outreach, include local corporations and utility companies on your press release mailing list. Many will include news of your volunteer outreach in their in-house employee publications or customer newsletters.

- In some communities, large food chains and retail operations support local nonprofit organizations by publishing information about their activities in their fliers or placing announcements in their stores. Explore these possibilities in your community.

- Survey your volunteers to find out whether they are affiliated with any faith group or civic or social organization that might be a good candidate for a presentation on your volunteer program. Ask them to make the contact or refer you to someone who can.

- Weekly neighborhood newspapers are an often overlooked, yet valuable, resource to help you reach prospective volunteers.

- If you want to generate a feature story about your recruitment outreach, appoint some volunteer leaders for your campaign. Send a press release about those appointments to the neighborhood weekly in the areas in which these volunteers live. Include a contact number to set up an interview and to obtain details about your volunteer outreach program.

- By cultivating relationships with local media professionals, when a need arises for promotion, like a volunteer recruitment campaign, you will already have contacts in place.

- Consider inviting a press or media representative to join your board. This will not only give you a built-in contact, but access to professional advice on how to improve your media relations.

- In the course of carrying out your mission, always keep alert for possible situations that might generate interest in the development of a feature story about one of your volunteers.

- Getting one of your volunteers to host a dinner or weekend brunch for a group of their friends is an effective way to promote your volunteer program to a new group of potential volunteers.

- If you have a facility in which you provide services, there is an advantage to launching your recruitment outreach with an open house. This would give prospective volunteers an opportunity to see what services you offer. To generate a reason for people to come, and make the event newsworthy so the local press will cover it, use the open house to honor someone of note in the community who has been a friend to your organization.

- Remember, most people have an expectation that volunteering will be fun. Be sure to acknowledge this aspect of volunteering in all your recruitment presentations.

- Recruiting volunteers does not have to be an elaborate undertaking. It can be as simple as asking each of your volunteers to try to enlist one new volunteer, something that can be done any time during the year, with no expense except perhaps creating some printed material to give to prospective volunteers.

- To help your less experienced volunteers sharpen their presentation skills, pair them with a more skilled presenter until they develop the confidence and proficiency to take the lead or work on their own.

CHAPTER 5:

THE MEDIUM AND THE MESSAGE

In 1964, Marshall McLuhan published *Understanding Media: The Extension of Man*. In this seminal book about how we communicate, he proposed that the characteristic of the medium that delivers a message carries with it its own message. Or to quote the phrase he coined in the book: "The medium is the message."

The validity of McLuhan's observation has been born out dramatically over the past two decades with the dynamic upsurge in new technology. Today, the implications hold a special meaning for anyone looking to recruit volunteers, from Baby Boomers down to young volunteers. Your ability to determine the right medium for delivering your message to these two groups can mean the difference between successful recruiting and failure.

Volunteer Recruiting Today: The Challenges of a Wired World

Much has been written about the changing face of volunteerism in America. A recent study the AARP commissioned provides some insights on the subject. The study, carried out by Peter D. Hart Research Associates, in association with Civic Enterprise, focused on a diverse cross-section of Americans ages 44 to 79 — referred to by the researchers as "The Experienced Generation."

The researchers conducted a series of focus groups and a nation-wide telephone survey. Two of their findings are of particular interest to nonprofits seeking to recruit volunteers: four out of ten, or 41 percent of the people interviewed, said they were somewhat or very likely to increase the amount of time they spend volunteering in the next five years. Thirty-nine percent said they had retired and did increase their volunteer time.

Then there is the nationwide study conducted by the Corporation for

BY THE NUMBERS

41 percent of Americans age 44 to 79 say they are somewhat or very likely to increase the amount of time they volunteer in the next five years.

39 percent who have retired said they did increase their volunteer time.

55 percent to **29** percent. Young people 12 -18 volunteer at twice the rate of adults.

National and Community Service in conjunction with the U.S. Census Bureau and Independent Sector. This study revealed that 15.5 million young people between the ages of 12 and 18 contributed more than 1.3 billion hours of volunteer service in 2005. That means young people are volunteering at twice the rate of adults: 55 percent as compared to 29 percent. The report further states that 39 percent of the teenagers who volunteered were regular volunteers, compared with 55 percent of adult volunteers who fell in that category.

These two studies provide encouraging news for nonprofits, but tapping into this virtual goldmine created by the young generation and the Experienced Generation is going to require more than a traditional recruitment approach. Nonprofits are going to have to figure a way to recruit these potential volunteers where they live — and that is in a "wired" world.

Many nonprofits have already gotten the message. According to *The Journal of Volunteer Administration*, next to word-of-mouth, nonprofits list their website as their most useful volunteer recruiting strategy, followed by internet recruiting services. It is worth noting that the fourth most useful strategy in the list of ten was live presentations to groups, which was discussed in the last chapter.

Your website is the lynch pin in your box of cyber recruiting tools, but you have others. Anyone who has or knows a teenager understands the major role online social networking plays in their lives, and now it appears Baby Boomers are beginning to catch the fever. The DMN3 Institute, a market research company, conducted a study in 2015 of online social and professional networking by Boomers. Of their sample, 91 percent said they had visited social networks such as Facebook, Google+, and

Pinterest, as well as the online professional network, LinkedIn. Furthermore, 58 percent reported that they visited a company website, 57 percent continued to research further by using a search engine, and 51 percent liked, shared, or commented on a status update while using social media.

According to Marketingprofs.com, Boomers spend on average 19 hours a month online. Eighty-three percent of Boomers say the internet is their top source to learn about information. For a look at some of the sites customized to serve this demographic, type "Boomer" and "websites" into any search engine.

While research tells us younger people seem to prefer interactive sites and Boomers tend to use the web more for seeking information, there is no doubt that the internet plays an important role in the lives of both groups. The next question is how can you use this information to target the potential volunteers you want?

Your Website as a Recruitment Tool

Your most effective door into today's wired world is your website. As a recruitment tool, it offers several advantages. It is a tireless recruiter, available 24/7. No matter what time of day or night someone wants to check out information about your volunteer requirements or opportunities, the information is there, waiting for them. Website-based recruitment is reliable and gives you complete control over your recruitment message, which allows you to maintain consistency. Because you can make changes easily, you are able to keep your recruitment information up-to-date. Website-based recruitment can save you time and energy because it produces a replicable database on prospective volunteers, information that can be easily downloaded later to the individual's management file.

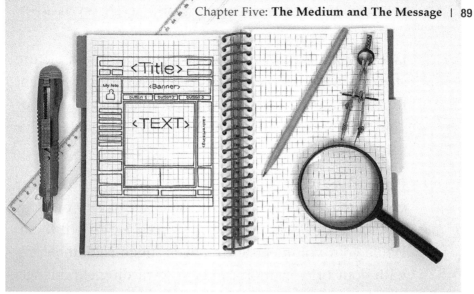

How effective the volunteer recruitment component of your website will be for you depends on how well you design it. Your volunteer recruitment page should be:

- **Easy to Access**: If someone is interested in volunteering for your organization he or she should not have to search through your whole website to find the information he or she needs. There should be an easy-to-spot link that takes him or her directly to your volunteering page with one click.

- **Attractive**: Too many nonprofits fail to fully develop the volunteering component of their website. If you want the viewer to explore your volunteering information, you need to make the page visually exciting and inviting.

- **Engaging:** One way to engage your prospective volunteer is with pictures and testimonials from your current volunteers. You can use head shots and printed statements, montages, or video. If the volunteer work you offer is visually interesting, take advantage of this. Generate excitement with picture stories or video of your volunteers in action. If you want to reach young people, have some young faces on your volunteer page. You might also want to add an interactive component for them.

- **Persuasive**: Just because someone has sought out your volunteer recruitment page does not mean they are sold on the idea of volunteering. It is your job to sell them. While your volunteer testimonials suggest volunteering with your organization can be a rewarding experience, somewhere on your volunteer recruitment page you should spell out — in print and with visuals — all the advantages of volunteering for your organization.

- **Easy to Use**: Once the prospective volunteer makes the decision to act, the next step — applying to become a volunteer — should be simple. Keep the process uncomplicated and easy to complete.

- **Responsive**: Whether you use a verifying email or have the prospective volunteers print out verification their application was received, the applicant should be given some record of the transaction. Your volunteer recruitment page should also contain contact information so prospective volunteers can follow up by phone or email to check the status of their application.

Information Your Volunteer Recruitment Page Needs to Include

In addition to listing specific volunteer opportunities or — if recruiting is an ongoing activity for your organization —

explaining your volunteer policy, you want to give potential volunteers a good reason to respond. Tell them about your mission, your program focus, how your work benefits the community, and, most importantly, how becoming a volunteer will benefit them.

Even if you have it elsewhere on your site, include the physical and email address and the phone number of your organization on your recruitment page. You do not want someone you have just sold on volunteering to have to search for this information, nor do you want him or her to have to wait to act on it. The quickest way to get them to act is to include a link on the page for signing up online. Or you could have a link that enables them to begin the sign-up process by emailing you.

To make the most of these procedures, be sure your organization is set up to respond to that email message or electronic application within two working days. This is not simply a matter of common courtesy. Enthusiasm tends to wane with time and the longer you wait to respond, the more you risk losing your potential volunteers, or at the very least, losing some of their trust. Your delay in responding could be interpreted as indifference, or a sign of ineptness.

If you are not set up for an electronic response, or find it more in keeping with your operation to have prospective volunteers contact you by telephone, you can make the process more convenient for the potential volunteer by posting the hours someone will be available to take their calls.

> "Asking for volunteers, but not responding to them immediately or not having a method to immediately place them into your program, is like advertising a product you don't really have, which can cause hard feelings about your agency on the part of potential supporters."
> — **ServiceLeader.org:** Virtual Volunteering

Sometimes there is no way to avoid using an answering machine, but even this experience can be made more volunteer-friendly. When you are recruiting, add a couple sentences to your organization's standard telephone message acknowledging you are currently accepting applications for volunteers. Invite any interested people to leave their number, assuring them the appropriate person will contact them. Again, you should make every effort to have someone respond to their message within 48 hours.

First impressions do count. The first person from your organization your prospective volunteer meets, in person or on the phone, can shape your whole relationship with that volunteer. Do a little preliminary work; make sure whoever is answering your phones knows you are recruiting volunteers and is able to answer basic questions about your volunteer program. Let them know how important their interaction with prospective volunteers is. Encourage them to be friendly and accommodating.

Being able to apply for your volunteer program through your website is both convenient and time saving for the potential volunteer, but it does not negate the value of a personal contact. Whether someone has applied online, by email, or by calling your offices and leaving a message, they should get a follow-up call from someone involved with your recruitment program, someone who will thank them for their interest and answer any questions they may have.

Email as a Recruiting Tool

Does your donor or volunteer base give you access to email addresses? If you are a religious organization or professional group, do you communicate with your members by email? Do you have contacts with organizations that share your mission and would be willing to email their members about your volunteer needs? If the answer is yes to any of these questions, email can be another effective tool for getting your volunteer recruitment message out.

Barbara Howard, who coordinates volunteers for the Tampa Bay Bird Stewarding Project on Florida's Gulf Coast, puts email to good use in her volunteer recruitment effort.

VOLUNTEER STORIES
FROM THE FIELD

Friends of the Tampa Bay National
Wildlife Refuges Bird Steward Program
Tampa, Florida
b-howard2001@msn.com

The Friends of Tampa Bay National Wildlife Refuges, a 501(c)(3) nonprofit volunteer organization, provides assistance to and supports programs of the U.S. Fish & Wildlife Service. Barbara Howard coordinates the activities of a fluctuating corps of volunteers who act as bird stewards, monitoring and protecting the terns, laughing gulls, black skimmers, and other birds that nest on the area's refuge islands and beaches.

Report from Barbara Howard, founder and coordinator of the Bird Steward Program of the Friends of Tampa Bay National Wildlife Refuges.

Our group, Friends of the Tampa Bay National Wildlife Refuges, has been successful in recruiting volunteers from like-minded groups. For example, Audubon members are interested in birds and our national wildlife refuges in Tampa Bay are set aside for birds. The folks in Audubon are very willing to help protect birds on the refuges. We recruit volunteers at local festivals by having displays showing what we do as well as talking to people about the volunteer opportunities we have. We also contact local colleges to find out if they have students in need of volunteer hours. In every case we try to get an email and phone number from prospective volunteers.

Most people these days have an email that they check at least weekly. Using emails to contact volunteers when a volunteer opportunity is coming up is an easy way to mobilize many volunteers. It would be logistically impossible to call every prospective volunteer and cost prohibitive to send out notices by mail, therefore email is quick, easy, and inexpensive. We successfully mobilize 16 to 25 volunteers each weekend day during the summer for our bird steward program.

We have a website for the group that has a section for volunteer opportunities and will most likely open a Facebook page in the near future.

SAMPLE OF ACTUAL VOLUNTEER RECRUITMENT EMAIL FOR BIRD STEWARDS SENT BY COLLABORATING ASSOCIATION

Subject: Can't steward during the day? Please help out at night as an *evening steward*:

Beach nesting bird locations at Indian Shores (Suncoast Seabird Sanctuary), Treasure Island (Sunset Beach), and Clearwater Beach need our help this holiday weekend especially from *8:30pm till around 11pm/midnight*. People caught up in the 4th of July spirit head to the beaches to shoot off fireworks. This scares the parent birds away and leaves the chicks confused and running about. We try to keep the chicks close to home in the roped off areas. We also make sure people don't shoot their fireworks toward the colony.

Please come help on July 3 & 4th at any of these beaches from 8:30pm til it stops.

Contact Barb Howard at b_howard2001@msn.com <mailto:b_howard2001@msn.com> or call 727 343-1272 or 727 512-4914 cell to volunteer.

We also need *daytime stewards *every weekend at most or all of our locations well into August. I still have the following openings for this holiday weekend:

July 3rd, Friday
Ft DeSoto afternoon
Indian Shores afternoon and 8:30pm shift
Sunset Beach morning, afternoon, or all day, and 8:30pm shift
Shell Key 10-4
Clearwater Beach 8:30pm shift

July 5th, Sunday
Indian Shores, Sunset Beach, and Clearwater Beach - just a few people for the 8:30 shift — not sure if people will still be shooting fireworks.

The bird stewarding is really helping — we actually have Least Terns nesting on the public beaches!!!! When they don't get disturbed by humans, they can succeed on the beaches.

All of the locations have absolutely wonderful opportunities for seeing Florida birds and chicks! Please help out in protecting them.
Barb
--
Beth Forys, PhD
Professor of Environmental Studies & Biology
Eckerd College

As with a press release, keep your email brief, cover basic facts, and provide accurate contact information. You should also invite the recipient to share the information with friends, family, and anyone else they think might be interested in volunteering.

If you have set up a speakers program as a part of your recruitment outreach, include this information in your email, with a request for the recipient to inform you if they know of any organization that might be interested in having a presentation. Encourage response by adding an email link for their reply.

Online Social and Professional Networking as a Recruiting Tool

Research formerly indicated that unless you are looking for volunteers under 30, your results will not warrant the effort required. However, there are indications that this is in the process of changing. The latest research shows that even the Baby Boomer generation is online now; as we mentioned before, 91 percent claim to use one or more social media sites regularly.

More and more nonprofit websites are including links to OSN platforms. For Jane Davis, founder of Hope-Howse, a New Mexico-based grassroots volunteer organization, Facebook has proven to be, in her

"Having [your supporters] like your page on Facebook or follow you on Twitter provides an opportunity to appear on their feeds and give them daily reminders of your mission. Social media is a great tool to help drive traffic to your website, and subsequently attract donations, volunteers, and raise general awareness for your cause."

— Manoverboard.com

words, "an incredible connector." She reports that she currently has some 300 "friends" (contacts) on the OSN platform, and says it has been a help in recruiting people of all ages. To underline her belief that Facebook is no longer just for the under-30 crowd, she points out that her father, who is 83, is active on Facebook.

One organization that has incorporated OSN platforms, YouTube, and even Twitter into their ongoing recruitment program with great success is the American Cancer Society.

 **VOLUNTEER STORIES FROM THE FIELD**

 The American Cancer Society®
Atlanta, GA
Website: **www.cancer.org**

In addition to their websites, the American Cancer Society uses all available forms of social networking to recruit and mobilize a volunteer community of nearly three million. Their success attracting and maintaining volunteers is due in part to their willingness to maintain constant presence on these platforms.

Report from Laura Reeves, chief talent officer, American Cancer Society

Mobilizing volunteers is about community presence. For today's volunteer, this presence is increasing through social media and e-communities. The American Cancer Society is committed to being visible and accessible to people where they choose to gather, and making it as easy as possible for people to get involved in the fight against cancer to save lives. That means rallying communities to fight back online.

People can find information about volunteering on the American Cancer Society's website (**www.cancer.org**), as well as American Cancer Society Facebook, MySpace, YouTube, and Twitter pages. From participating in a virtual American Cancer Society Relay for Life event in Second Life, to offering words of encouragement and hope to survivors and caregivers through our online support community (Cancer Survivor's Network), the American Cancer Society's online tools and resources allow people to save lives while fulfilling their own. Those interested in fighting back against cancer can even find "minute volunteering" opportunities on **www.cancer.org** that enable volunteers to get involved from their computer in just a matter of minutes. The American Cancer Society provides current volunteers access to a volunteer welcome center on the Society's intranet, which encourages participation on its social networks and through other opportunities. Additionally, people can find personal stories from current volunteers about why they get engaged and stay engaged with the American Cancer Society on **www.cancer.org**.

The American Cancer Society commits considerable manpower and time to its OSN recruiting outreach, and it is paying off for them. But they are a large operation with considerable resources. The question you need to ask yourself as you contemplate using OSN platforms for recruitment is whether the time and manpower required will be worth the return you will get on your investment.

First, there is the time to set up your organization's profile on the platform. Is someone in your organization going to have to learn how to do this, or do you have a staff member already well versed in OSN or OPN procedures? Once you have your profile set up, to be of any value the site will need to be checked and updated frequently. Who is going to monitor and keep it current? Are you comfortable with letting someone on your staff take time away from their other duties to do this, or do you have a volunteer who could take on this responsibility? Would you be able to garner a sufficient number of new volunteers from the platform to warrant the expenditure of this time?

The person managing your social media presence, whether an employee or volunteer, should be encouraged to present an upbeat and varied approach to his or her posts. Both upcoming and successfully completed events can be highlighted, as well as short blurbs about those involved with the organization. Appeals for volunteers or donations of all kinds can be brought to light. Inspirational quotes related to the genre of the organization can pique a reader's interest. An item on any social media site featuring a visual will garner more attention; make sure a photograph or fun graphic is attached to every posting.

A key characteristic in your OSN presence should be intentionality. Each post should bring awareness to the cause at the heart of the organization. Supporters and the general public alike should be directed to where they can find out more information about volunteering or donating to the organization. Creating a calendar in advance of dates, times, and types of posts will be beneficial, especially if more than one person is helping with this aspect of marketing.

There is a different, less time-consuming way you could use these platforms for recruiting volunteers. Instead of creating your own profile on a platform, you can request help from some of your volunteers who are already using OSN platforms. Ask your volunteers to list their volunteer activity as part of their profile, and request they post information about your need for volunteers on their OSN blog or announcement area. While this will eliminate the set-up time for using an OSN, you are still going to want to monitor the site to see what is being said about your organization. The time these actions take need to be factored into your decision.

On the downside, if you put your recruitment message onto a volunteer's OSN profile, you will have no control over the environment in which your message will appear. There is always the risk that there will be information in your volunteer's profile or on the site that your organization would rather not be associated with. Because your volunteer, not you or someone on your staff, will be posting the information, there is also the possibility your message will be distorted or contain inaccuracies that could cause problems later.

Online Recruiting Help

Thanks to the internet, the long-standing concept of centers that connect volunteers with nonprofits has morphed into a modern phenomenon, a variety of internet-driven organizations with the same mission, but now armed with sophisticated technology that enables them to connect volunteers and nonprofits — not just locally, but across the nation and around the world. These organizations include VolunteerMatch®, Volunteer Solutions, Serve Net, Idealist, Online Volunteering, UniversalGiving, and the Points of Light Foundation's Volunteer Center National Network.

One of the reasons for the growing success of these online organizations is their ability to fit into the busy lives of people who would like to volunteer, but who have neither the time nor knowledge to find a nonprofit with a mission that matches their interests or concerns. These organizations make the search simple. People can check these websites whenever it is convenient for them, see what is available in their area, have confidence that the organizations listed have been checked out and are legitimate, and offer their services on a schedule that fits with their lifestyle.

For nonprofits there are many benefits to working with an organization that offers online recruiting. These organizations give a nonprofit access to a broader, more diverse audience for its recruitment message than it could reach on its own, usually with no financial outlay. Because these web-based organizations help for-profit corporations develop volunteer programs for their employees, they are able to give nonprofits access to this valuable demographic of potential volunteers. There is another benefit. Most of these web-based recruitment organizations prescreen the volunteers who register with them; this increases the chance that volunteers recruited through this process will be a good fit for the nonprofit. Let us look at a few of these web-based organizations.

VolunteerMatch

VolunteerMatch is a pioneer in web-based recruitment; it was the first organization to establish a website that enables prospective volunteers nationwide to find volunteer opportunities from a vast, updated, locally organized computerized data base of active opportunities. According to its website, VolunteerMatch "strengthens communities by making it easier for good people and good causes to connect."

Director of Communications, Robert Rosenthal, reports that since the site was launched in 1998, nonprofit involvement has continuously grown. Today more than 109,000 nonprofits use the site for recruitment, with 250 to 300 new nonprofits applying for free membership to use the service every week. VolunteerMatch's nonprofit clients include such organizations as the American Red Cross^SM, the National Multiple Sclerosis Society, Habitat for Humanity®, Easter Seals®, and the Senior Corps. Many of the national nonprofits use VolunteerMatch to help their local affiliates recruit and manage their volunteers. VolunteerMatch also serves more than 100 corporate clients with employee volunteer programs and consumer volunteer engagement initiatives, making millions of additional volunteers available to its network of participating nonprofits.

> "VolunteerMatch is appealing and responsive to potential volunteers who have divergent backgrounds and interests, as well as wide ranging schedules and time available to commit to volunteering."
>
> — *How the Internet has Changed Volunteering: Findings from a VolunteerMatch User Study*

Both nonprofits and volunteers register by ZIP code. A multi-ZIP code feature allows nonprofits to list opportunities in targeted locations, and the Community Leader service provides for extended management. VolunteerMatch also offers online training in volunteer recruitment and management on their site. To check out the full scope of their services, go to their website: **www.volunteermatch.org**

Volunteer Solutions

Volunteer Solutions is a volunteer matching application that connects volunteers, nonprofit agencies, corporations, event organizers, and volunteer centers. Volunteers go to the site to find opportunities in their geographic region that match their interests or skills. They can check the list of available volunteer opportunities or enter a keyword. Individuals can also register on the site to receive automatic emails that list volunteer opportunities matching their profile. For nonprofits the site is a free recruiting resource, offering a partially screened, regionally separated list of potential volunteers to draw from.

Like VolunteerMatch, Volunteer Solutions services corporations seeking to promote volunteerism among their employees, therefore providing nonprofits with an opportunity to recruit volunteers from this desirable demographic. For more information on Volunteer Solutions go to their website: **www. volunteer.united-e-way.org**

UniversalGiving

UniversalGiving's website describes the organization as a marketplace that allows people to volunteer and donate to top performing projects in more than 70 countries around the world. Volunteers can search the website for projects by issue or region. More than 7,000 people have volunteered through UniversalGiving since it was launched in June of 2002.

Most of the NGOs UniversalGiving works with are hands-on, specifically focused international operations that respond to pressing human and environmental issues caused by natural disasters or economic instability. Among the organizations they serve are Global Aware, the GVN Foundation, Earthwatch Institute™, Hands to Heart International, and Relief International's Global Citizenship and Youth Philanthropy (GCYP).

According to CEO Pamela Hawley, "UniversalGiving uses a quality-control model to identify eligible nonprofits, assess whether their underlying idea and business plan are sound, and determine how well they are executing against that plan." Whenever possible, they seek recommendations from experts and meet with management teams. It is this rigorous quality control, Hawley says, that enables UniversalGiving to assure donors and volunteers that the organizations they are helping are legitimate, and that their time or money is being well invested.

Whether you are an international nonprofit or a national or local charity, UniversalGiving's process for vetting volunteers can be instructive.

VOLUNTEER STORIES FROM THE FIELD

Website: **www.UniversalGiving.org**

Report from Pamela Hawley, CEO, UniversalGiving

Volunteers are not free. They are valuable, skilled, talented people who deserve proper management and communications, just as any paid team member. Nonprofits need to invest time and resources into these volunteers to give them the respect and guidance needed to operate well in their volunteer positions. Equally important, the nonprofit must reach a balance between the goals of its organization and the goals of the volunteer. It is important that the organization reach its goals, but it is also essential that the volunteer feels that their own personal goals are being met.

One of the ways we do this is through a job description. We speak with the volunteer about what our goals are, and what they would like to do. Then we provide them with a template of a job description, so they have the format. The volunteer then creates his or her own job description, pointing out specific areas of interest — usually three to five, as they may work on multiple projects. This gives the volunteer a sense of ownership in the creation of their position, and it also allows us to know that we were heard appropriately about UniversalGiving's goals. If you just hand the job description to a volunteer it doesn't create a sense of ownership or demonstrate good organizational listening skills. After we receive the job description, we provide constructive feedback, usually on priorities and what is emphasized most.

Recruiting volunteers on the Web is a great way to find a good match. And volunteers have a sense of ownership when they search the web. They have the opportunity to decide the issue they care about, the location, the schedule/hours, the size of the organization, the type of team they want to work with. All of this can be vetted before they walk in the door.

Virtual Volunteering

"Never be afraid to do something new. Remember amateurs built the ark, professionals built the Titanic."

— Anonymous

A rape crisis center is petitioning the legislature, but needs background information on the issue. A church is looking for volunteer help to design and write an online newsletter. A food bank is running short of food and needs someone to contact commercial food distributors to see if they will donate some of their product. A community theater is looking for someone to check online for possible grants. A small nonprofit needs help with its database. These are all things that can be done by a virtual volunteer.

Virtual volunteers, also known as online volunteers, are people who do their volunteering from home using the internet. They may be people who prefer to volunteer from home or someone with a disability for whom on-site volunteering is not possible. There are also people who volunteer both on-site and virtually. Virtual volunteers offer nonprofits one more way to augment staff resources and expand their outreach capabilities and they do this without impinging on the nonprofit's often limited workspace.

Virtual volunteering has grown considerably in the past ten years, and improved technology is partly responsible for the growth. Another contributor may be the recent downturn in the economy. Working from home gives people an opportunity to volunteer without incurring travel expenses, which could put a strain on their already-strapped finances. It also allows people to fit volunteering more easily into their busy schedules.

Nonprofits are currently using virtual volunteers for such things as fundraising, translation, research, computer assistance, data processing, graphic design, social media management, and web development. Online volunteers are also serving as mentors for school children. Churches are using them for evangelical work. Because virtual volunteers work from home, it does not matter where they live. If a nonprofit needs a particular skill it can recruit a virtual volunteer to fill that need from anywhere in the country, or even abroad, if necessary.

Virtual Volunteering – Getting Started

Virtual volunteering is not a substitute for traditional volunteering, it is an adjunct to it; it provides nonprofits with another recruitment tool and an additional source of volunteers. Before you can begin setting up a virtual volunteer program, you need to have all the policies and procedures in place that make a traditional volunteer program work smoothly, many of which have already been discussed. They will be the foundation upon which you will build your virtual volunteer program. However, there are some critical differences between recruiting and managing volunteers on-site and managing virtual volunteers. Fortunately, help is just a click away. There are two excellent resources that can get you started and support you as you delve into the world of virtual volunteering. They can, fittingly, be found online.

The Virtual Volunteering Project

In 1996, **www.serviceleader.org** launched The Virtual Volunteering Project. The objective of the project was to encourage the development of volunteer activities that can be completed off-site, and to provide help to nonprofits wishing to engage in this type of volunteering. This cutting-edge concept has grown into an internationally recognized resource conducted online today by volunteers and program managers from all over the world. For anyone interested in setting up a virtual volunteer program, this site offers information, workshops, resources, and other types of help. To learn more about the Virtual Volunteer Project, log on to **www.serviceleader.org/vv.**

The Virtual Volunteering Guidebook

The Virtual Volunteering Guidebook: How to Apply the Principals of Real-World Volunteer Management to Online Service is a 138 page, full color PDF document created by Susan J. Ellis and Jayne Cravens. Ellis, president of Energize, Inc., is an internationally renowned expert on volunteerism. She has written or co-authored nine books and more than 70 articles on volunteer management. Cravens, a former manager of the Virtual Volunteer Project, has presented numerous workshops on virtual volunteering, online outreach, using online technology, and similar subjects. The guidebook covers every aspect of preparing for, recruiting, and managing virtual volunteers, and can be read online or downloaded free from the website. To learn more, log on to **www.serviceleader.org/new/virtual** and click The Virtual Volunteering Guidebook.

Incorporating New Technologies

There are two free resources that can help you determine if you are ready to add new technology to your recruitment and management plan. A checklist — "Stages of Maturity in Non Profit Organizations: Use of Online Technology" — can be found online at **www.coyotecommunications.com/outreach/ online3.html.** You can use the list to help you determine your organization's degree of technical maturity, and what changes you might need to make to enable you to take advantage of the new technologies available today. Another free resource to help you evaluate your organization's readiness is "Technology Literacy Benchmarks for Nonprofit Organizations," a PDF file published by the Benton Foundation and NPower available at **www.benton.org/publibrary/stratcom/techlit.pdf**.

If you determine your organization is ready to begin using new technologies, a resource that can help you get started is **www. techsoup.org.** This website provides how-to articles, worksheets, and product comparisons written for nonprofits of all levels of technical expertise and sizes. The website also provide free webinars — a form of web conferencing — and other learning events, and offers access to donated and discounted technology products from companies such as Microsoft®, Adobe®, and Symantec®.

Technology is an invaluable recruitment tool. Explore it, use it, but never forget that it is only a tool. To be successful, a recruitment outreach must be carefully planned and executed using whatever tools or resources will help you reach your organization's recruitment goals, which are always determined by your specific volunteer needs. This book covers many of these possible tools and resources, but you may discover more as you put your recruitment plan into action. Do not be afraid to explore other possibilities or approaches. If you stay focused on your goals and measure all your ideas by that standard, you will not go wrong.

Some Tips on Recruiting Volunteers in a Wired World

- Your most effective tool for reaching the "wired generation" is your online presence. One item in your technological toolbox is your organization's website. It also makes a powerful statement about your organization and can positively or negatively reinforce your brand.

- While many word processing programs provide templates for setting up a website, given its importance and all you need it to do, it may pay to invest in professional help.

- If your funds are limited, see if you have a volunteer or group of volunteers with the skills to set up your website.

- Ensure your website is a good salesman for your volunteer program. Tell the viewer about the joy and the satisfaction they will receive if they volunteer with your organization.

- Young people tend to be savvier about computers and websites. Do not overlook your younger volunteers or the children of volunteers if you need help in setting up or maintaining yours.

- You want your website to be attractive and stand out, but a top priority should be ease of use.

- Much research has been written on the psychology and design principles behind good website design — what people look at first, how the eye travels across the screen, etc. Do some research so you know how to prioritize your information by location on the page, alignment, contrast, and proximity. Two books that might be helpful are "Designing Visual Interfaces: Communication Oriented Techniques" by Kevin Mullet and Darrel Sano and "Site-Seeing: A Visual Approach to Web Usability" by Stephen Few.

- There should be an easy-to-spot link on your main page that enables a viewer to reach your volunteer information with one click.

- Volunteer testimonials on your website will provide persuasive evidence that volunteering with your organization will be a good experience for your prospective volunteer.

- A picture is worth 1,000 words, especially when the picture shows happy volunteers at work.

- Be sure to update your website frequently. Keep it fresh so returning visitors will always find something new to draw them into the site. This is especially true for your volunteer page. People seldom make a decision the first time they receive information. You want to re-engage the potential volunteer every time they come back until they make their decision to volunteer.

- The web is an immediate gratification medium. When someone clicks on to your volunteer page, take advantage of this. Give them something to smile about; something that gives them a good feeling and makes them want to stay.

- Make language work for you. The word "volunteer" can sound impersonal. Do not be afraid to use words like "pitch in" or "help out" on your volunteer page.

- If people sign up to volunteer on your website, make sure someone responds within two working days. Wait longer than that, and you could lose your prospective volunteer, or at the very least, their respect.

- There is no use selling someone on volunteering if you do not give them an easy way to act on the desire you create. Keep the process of signing up quick and simple.

- First impressions do count. Invest some time in preparing the individual who will be receiving a potential volunteer's first phone call. Make sure they are knowledgeable about your volunteer program and aware of how their behavior will reflect on your organization.

- Before you add OSN platforms to your recruiting tool kit, take the time to be deliberate about this aspect of your outreach. Take into consideration the time and manpower required to set them up and maintain them. Plan ahead to make sure your social media presence will help you reach the demographics you want to target for your volunteer program.

- Instead of setting up a profile for your organization on an OSN platform, consider enlisting the help of volunteers who are already established on one of these platforms. Ask them to post information about your volunteer needs on the site for you.

- When and if you do create a social media presence, make sure it is intentional. Keep in mind that varying the types of posts that will be crafted will hold your audience's interest. Research what time of day and even what day of the week are best to obtain the highest level of visibility from your audience. Use visuals — for example, pictures of your volunteers happily serving will help inspire others to join the cause, while charts and graphs can provide valuable information to potential volunteers and donors.

- Email can be an excellent recruiting tool for an organization that has access to a pertinent email data base from its own organization, or through organizations with compatible interests. A food bank may ask churches in the area to send emails to all their members about the food bank's need for volunteers. Or a bird stewarding program could use the email network of environmental organizations to get the word out that they are looking for volunteers.

- Online volunteer recruitment organizations like VolunteerMatch or Volunteer Solutions can help nonprofits reach a broader audience than they could reach on their own.

- Nonprofits who would like to tap into the corporate workplace for volunteers can either contact local corporations directly, or enlist the help of online volunteer recruiting organizations. For direct contact, the person whom you should approach depends on the structure of the organization or your community contacts. Your contacts in the community might be able to put you directly in touch with the CEO or another corporate officer or board member. In some cases, it might be best to go through the human resources department, or the community relations department. If you have a volunteer who works for the organization, he or she may be your best connection. It may take a little research but the quality of volunteer this type of recruiting produces is worth the effort.

- Virtual volunteering offer nonprofits one more way to augment staff resources and expand their outreach capabilities without impinging on the nonprofit's limited workspace.

- Before you can begin adding virtual volunteers as a resource, you need to make sure you have built a solid recruitment and management foundation for your on-site volunteers.

- There are major differences in recruiting and managing on-site volunteers and virtual volunteers. Two sources of help are *The Virtual Volunteer Project* and *The Virtual Volunteer Handbook* by Susan J. Ellis and Jayne Cravens. Both can be found online at **www.serviceleader.org.**

- Volunteer recruitment should be a creative venture. All possibilities should be considered, and all available tools or concepts should be explored. What you eventually end up using should be determined exclusively by what, in this plethora of possibilities, will best help you meet your recruitment goals.

CHAPTER 6:

BRINGING NEW VOLUNTEERS ONBOARD

You have spent considerable time and effort recruiting and you have found a number of possible qualified candidates. Now you are faced with a new challenge — deciding whom to accept and where to place them. How you approach this depends on your recruitment goals.

There are occasions when the "warm-body" approach to recruiting makes sense: if you are recruiting for a one-time event, for example, and need a large number of people to perform tasks that require no special skills. While you would need to consider your organization's risk management policies as you screen your candidates, because of the short-term nature of the volunteer service and the low level of skill needed, there would be no need for rigorous screening.

However, the majority of nonprofits are looking for a different kind of volunteer. The volunteers they seek will interact with staff or clients and are being recruited to meet specific, predetermined needs. In these situations, a more discerning selection process is necessary. A key component of this process is the personal interview.

> "Volunteer interviewing consists of evaluating a person for a job, not the job."
>
> — Steve McCurley, Posted 4/2004, **www.Casanet.org**

There are significant differences between interviewing someone for a paying job and interviewing someone for a volunteer position. A job interview may take into consideration the candidate's ability to fit into the corporate culture, but its primary focus is on filling the job. The focus of a volunteer screening interview is on the candidate. The interviewer's primary concern is to find an appropriate placement within the organization for the potential volunteer. Therefore determining how the candidate will fit into the nonprofit's culture becomes not just an after-thought but a major consideration. This difference in focus calls for a specific, behavior-based style of interviewing that requires an understanding of psychology and human nature.

Preparing for the Interview

The volunteer recruitment interview is designed to accomplish three things:

- Enable the interviewer to evaluate the potential volunteers' interests, skills, and temperament in order to determine their suitability for the organization and match them with an appropriate job.

- Reinforce the potential volunteers' decision to volunteer, and assure them that their services will be valued by the organization.

- Convince the potential volunteers that their volunteering experience will be fun and bring them personal satisfaction.

Even individuals who have gone through the interview process many times find it stressful, so you want to do everything you can to make your interview with your potential volunteer as comfortable as possible. Establishing that sense of comfort begins with your choice of a location for the interview. You want a pleasant, private, quiet, and easily accessible setting. The ambiance of the room should be friendly and welcoming. You are not simply conducting an interview; you are beginning a relationship. The sense of comfort you establish during this initial contact sends a message to your prospective volunteer that they will be comfortable in your organization. Even if you cannot find a place for the candidate, you still want the interview to be a good experience so they will continue to support your organization.

Interviewer's Tool Kit

- Candidate's completed application or questionnaire

- List of available volunteer positions and skills required

- Background on organization's volunteer policy

- Handouts on organization's history, mission, focus

- A list of open-ended questions to generate conversation that will help interviewer assess the candidate and fit him or her to an available position

Accomplishing these interview goals requires preparation. The interviewers need to familiarize themselves with the information the candidates provided on their recruitment questionnaire, and they need to be knowledgeable about the volunteer positions that must be filled and the skills and attitudes necessary to effectively fill them. Interviewers also need to be sensitive to the organization's culture: Do the current volunteers tend to socialize, or do they come in, do their job, and then leave? Do the

organization's most successful volunteers exhibit characteristics that the interviewer should look for in the candidates? Is there a need for more diversity? These are some of the things the interviewers need to consider in preparing their interview questions, always keeping in mind that the conversation with the candidate will generate new questions they have not prepared for.

The interview should begin with a few informal direct questions to put the candidate at ease. Based on the questionnaire the candidate filled out, the interviewer might ask the candidate about his or her family, job, interests, or affiliations. Building on these informal questions, the interviewer will switch to open-ended, behavior-based questions designed to generate a conversation that will reveal the candidate's attitude, temperament, and style of dealing with situations. It is these questions that will help the interviewer determine how, where, or even if the candidate will fit into the organization.

The purpose of using behavior-based interviewing is to find out how the interviewee reacted in a specific situation. The logic here is that how someone behaved in the past is a good predictor of how they will behave in the future. If you give your candidate a hypothetical situation and ask what he or she would do, chances are the answer you will get is the answer he or she thinks you want. But if you get your candidate talking about a situation he or she actually experienced, and ask him or her how they handled the situation, you will gain insight into how they might handle a similar situation if it arose during their volunteer experience.

This type of interviewing requires patience, sensitivity, a deep understanding of your organization and its mission, and exceptional listening skills. It also usually requires special training. Ideally, to conduct your screening interviews you would have someone professionally trained in this type of interviewing. However, if your organization is not able to afford professionally trained individuals for the task, look for and cultivate these abilities in the individuals you entrust with this critical responsibility. There are consultants who can be employed to train staff members. Free help is available through websites such as **Energizeinc.com** and **VolunteerMatch.org**.

The Interview

The interviewer — armed with information about the available volunteer positions; handouts on the organization and its volunteer program; the candidate's completed questionnaire; and the list of conversation-starting, open-ended questions — is now ready to meet with a potential volunteer. The interviewing process might go something like this:

- The interviewer welcomes the candidate and thanks him or her for coming. A cup of coffee or tea or a cold drink might be offered to put him or her at ease.

- Before launching into the interview, the interviewer engages the candidate in casual conversation — based on the candidate's completed questionnaire — about his or her family, interests, affiliations, or the reason he or she decided to volunteer.

- Once the conversational style of the interview has been established, the interviewer explains the purpose of the meeting and provides background on the organization and how the volunteer program works. The candidate is encouraged to ask questions and express his or her views on this information. Then the open-ended behavior-based questions are introduced.

- At this point in the interview, the nature of the organization and the type of volunteers being sought comes into play. If you are looking for help with office work, the candidate's office skills would be explored. If the volunteer positions will involve dealing with clients, past experience with the kind of skills the position requires become more important, as does the candidate's temperament and character.

- When the interviewer is satisfied that the individual is suitable for one or more of the open volunteer positions, these positions are discussed in detail, including the setting and the nature of the work the volunteer will be asked to do.

- Sometimes volunteers come in with a specific kind of position in mind. The interviewer, aware of the organization's needs, might see skills or an aptitude that would suit the candidate for another type of position. While the candidate should be made aware of this position, the issue should not be pressed if they show no interest. Volunteers are more likely to stay with an organization if the work they do fits in with their interests. It would be more productive to continue looking until you find a position the candidate would be interested in.

- When the interviewer is ready to offer the candidate a position, all aspects of the commitment the volunteer is being asked to accept should be discussed. The interviewer should explain in detail the time commitment involved, training requirements, orientation, confidentiality and safety policies, and any other pertinent information related to the position or the experience the volunteer will have.

- After the volunteer is given all the details about the position, the interviewer needs to confirm that the volunteer will be able to do the job: How many hours a week is he or she available? Does he or she have access to reliable transportation? Is he or she willing to commit to the time frame expected? How soon can he or she start? Only after all these details are settled is the volunteer offered the position.

- The interviewer concludes the interview by thanking the new volunteer and explaining what comes next — orientation, the timeline for training, when he or she can expect to begin.

The scenario above is just an example of how an interview session might go. In actual practice the structure and content of the screening interview will be shaped by your organization's nature and volunteer needs. The effectiveness of your interview process will depend on the skill of your interviewers.

When a Candidate is Rejected

There will be occasions when an interviewer may have to turn away a candidate. The interviewing process may have revealed  this individual's temperament was not suitable for any of the available volunteer positions, or the interviewer may have uncovered a hidden agenda that would be disruptive to the organization's culture. Sometimes a recruitment campaign goes so well that an organization inadvertently over-recruits, and there are not enough positions for the number of qualified applicants who apply. The challenge now is to find a way to gracefully reject the candidate without creating ill feelings toward your organization.

Some smaller organizations prefer to deliver the news that the candidate's services will not be needed by telephone. This is also frequently the case if the interviewer or someone in the organization knows the candidate personally. In most instances, however, the rejection is handled in a letter. In either situation the rejection needs to be presented in a manner that does not suggest the candidate is being personally rejected.

A rejection letter should be formal, but friendly. Thank the candidate for taking the time to come in for an interview. Express your pleasure at having the opportunity to meet him or her and acknowledge the skills, talents or, at the very least, the enthusiasm the individual has shown for your organization. Explain while there are no suitable volunteer positions available at the moment, his or her interest and his or her continued support of your organization and its mission are deeply appreciated. If appropriate, tell him or her that you will keep them in mind for a position in the future.

The Volunteer Manager

Before an organization can bring volunteers on board, it needs to have someone ready to manage them. That person will need strong administrative and organizational skills to coordinate and track all volunteer activity. He or she needs to understand budgeting because nonprofit volunteer programs always operate with financial constraints. Superior communication skills are essential —including the ability to be a good listener. People who manage volunteers should possess training and coaching skills so they can guide new volunteers as they take on unfamiliar responsibilities. Patience, flexibility, and a sense of humor are also invaluable traits in a volunteer manager.

Today, volunteer management is recognized as a profession; many colleges offer a degree in the subject. While more nonprofits are drawing their volunteer managers from a professional pool of these college graduates, some continue to appoint them from within the organization. A small nonprofit might place a staff member or a team of staff members in the role

"Directors of volunteer service need to be flexible. We seldom have privacy and are often interrupted ... even when it is not convenient. Volunteers like to share their stories and we need to take the time to listen."

— **Jane Lowe**, *director of Volunteer Service, Winthrop P. Rockefeller Cancer Institute at UAMS* of volunteer manager or coordinator, in which case they would balance this responsibility with their other work. Some small organizations rely on a volunteer to fill this position. Whether paid or volunteer, hired or appointed, to be effective a volunteer manager must receive support from management.

For a well-integrated volunteer program, a nonprofit needs to ensure its volunteer manager has ready access to its executive director, and meets regularly with its board of directors to keep them aware of volunteer activity. The volunteer manager's place in the nonprofit's hierarchy should reflect the vital role he or she plays in fulfilling the organization's mission.

A nonprofit must be a good steward of its resources, but it also needs to make sure the shepherd of one of its greatest resources — its volunteers — receives everything he or she needs to do the job. One of the soundest investments a nonprofit can make is in the training and continuing education and support of its volunteer manager. It is easy to forget how stressful this job can be, especially when your volunteer program appears to be running smoothly. However, juggling so many responsibilities and dealing with the broad spectrum of personalities a volunteer manager has to deal with every day can take its toll.

Networking with other volunteer managers through membership in organizations such as the Association of Leaders in Volunteer Engagement (AL!VE), attending volunteer management workshops, and taking time to utilizing online resources such as **www.Idealist.org** or **www.Energizeinc.com** helps keep a volunteer manager motivated, engaged, and prevents them from experiencing burnout. Continuing education and volunteer management support programs should be taken into consideration when preparing a volunteer management budget.

Orientation

By definition, orientation is a meeting or series of events at which introductory information or training is provided to somebody embarking on something new. It is a way to ensure your mission and work is clearly understood by all your volunteers. If you are looking for a long-term relationship with your new volunteers, however, your orientation needs to accomplish much more than this. You want the experience to leave your new volunteers confident they have made a good decision in choosing to volunteer with your organization. You want them to feel like a welcomed part of a team that shares an important mission, and excited about the adventure that lay ahead. This may sound like a tall order, but it is really a matter of introducing some old- fashioned rules of hospitality to the process.

How many times have you attended an event and found yourself wandering around a strange building trying to find where you were supposed to be? This is not how you want your new volunteers to begin their relationship with your organization. There should be someone on hand to greet them with a smile, acknowledge that they are expected, and direct them to wherever the orientation ceremony is being held. When they reach the meeting room, someone should greet them at the door and tell them how pleased they are to see them. There should be a nametag waiting for them.

According to media research, people relate to people and stories far more readily than they do to facts and figures.

If you want to reinforce the idea that you consider your new volunteers important, instead of traditional nametags, have a volunteer with some artistic ability write the names on the nametags and add art work to make them more attractive. Or you could go a step further and have personalized permanent nametags waiting for them suggesting your organization's expectation of a long and valued relationship with its new volunteers.

Too often the orientation ceremony is a perfunctory exercise. There is a formal welcoming speech, followed by a presentation about the history of the organization and a description of its mission and work. Charts are used to explain organizational structure, and there are discussions and handouts on policy and procedures, frequently provided in the form of a volunteer handbook. All these things are a necessary and important part of orientation, but they do not address one of the primary reasons people volunteer — social interaction. Your orientation also needs to address this expectation; it needs to allude to the relationship aspect of the volunteer experience.

One way to accomplish this is to include staff and board members in your orientation program. They should be introduced formally, but should also engage the new volunteers one-on-one before or after the formal presentation and make themselves available to answer questions.

Your experienced volunteers should also be invited to take part in your orientation. You might ask some of them to share a story about their volunteer experience as a part of the formal program. If you are a community service organization that engages therapists or counselors, you might include a presentation from them in your program. People relate to people and stories far more readily than they relate to facts and figures. And do not be afraid to include a little humor in your presentation to remind your new volunteers that they will be having fun while they are doing the good work they have volunteered to do.

Making Your New Volunteers Feel Comfortable

Unless your new volunteer is joining friends who already volunteer with your organization, they will most likely experience the normal discomfort one feels when thrust into a new, unfamiliar situation. Aside from providing a warm welcome, there are some other things you can do to make them comfortable:

• Precede the formal orientation presentation with a tour of the facility, including showing new volunteers where essential locations like the rest rooms, supply closets, and kitchen area are.

• Institute a buddy system for the orientation: Pair a new volunteer with an experienced volunteer or staff member — someone to put the new volunteer at ease and informally answer any questions they may have.

• A variation to the buddy system idea is to have an experienced volunteer or staff member personally guide two new volunteers through the orientation process. The advantage to this approach is that it gives the two new volunteers an opportunity to get to know each other as they share this unfamiliar process. There is something comforting about sharing a new experience with someone who is approaching it from the same perspective. This dual buddy system also creates the possibility that the two new volunteers will leave the orientation each having made a new friend.

• Before you begin the formal presentation, have each of the new volunteers stand up, introduce themselves, and briefly share a sentence or two about their background.

- If the number of new volunteers is small, the volunteer manager could present the new volunteers individually and provide some details about each person's background.

- The volunteer coordinator or the executive director of the organization could call up each of the new volunteers at the end of the orientation presentation and welcome them personally with a token present suitable to the mission of the organization. For example, a soup kitchen might present the standard apron volunteers use. If the campus is restricted, a parking sticker might be presented, or an identification card, or in the case of a hospital, the colored jacket that designates the individual as a volunteer worker — anything that suggests the new volunteer is officially now a part of the organization's volunteer team.

These are just a few suggestions on ways to incorporate the relationship aspect of volunteering into your orientation process. Think about your organization, how it functions, and the people in it who have a talent for telling your story, and you will probably come up with more ideas to make orientation a more valuable and memorable experience for your new volunteers.

Within a day or two after the orientation, the people who will be supervising your new volunteers should give them a courtesy call to thank them for attending the orientation and answer any questions they may have.

The Special Orientation Challenge for National Nonprofits

National not-for-profit organizations with multiple chapters and divisions face a special challenge when it comes to orientation:

consistency. How do you ensure all your volunteers who will receive their orientation from different people in different locations get the same correct and intended message about your mission and your work? The March of Dimes, with three million volunteers spread over 51 state chapters and 229 division offices throughout the United States, District of Columbia, and Puerto Rico, recently confronted and successfully resolved this issue.

VOLUNTEER STORIES
FROM THE FIELD

March of Dimes®

White Plains, New York

www.marchofdimes.com

The March of Dimes' mission is to improve the health of babies by preventing birth defects, premature birth, and infant mortality. According to the organization's mission statement, the March of Dimes' vision is "to become recognized as the foremost champion for babies, renowned as a great organization for volunteer leaders, and certified as a highly effective and efficient philanthropic organization." They use volunteers in every facet of their endeavor including research, education, advocacy and community service, and fundraising.

Report from Lauren Perlmutter, director, Volunteer Leadership Development

Volunteerism is critical to accomplishing our mission. March of Dimes welcomes and engages volunteers of diverse backgrounds, skills, and ages. We have limited staff, so we view volunteers as an expansion of our human resources. We have found that the development of a strong orientation program coupled with periodic training sessions covering specific March of Dimes leadership issues, such as the role and responsibility of our volunteer leaders, has helped us enormously.

As a result of our annual volunteer leadership survey, it became clear that many of our volunteers had not received a comprehensive orientation about the March of Dimes, creating inconsistency between chapter volunteer knowledge. This led to a major effort to develop an integrated, consistent orientation program. The program was designed in three parts — a 21-minute DVD entitled *The Power is You*; a self-study website (**http://ResourceCenter.MarchofDimes.com**); and an in-person customized local orientation presentation that could be conducted by the local chapter.

This kind of consistent in-depth orientation has led to our volunteer leaders becoming more articulate spokespersons for the March of Dimes and it has helped them better perform their volunteer roles.

The New Volunteers' First Day

Orientation introduced your new volunteers to an overview of your organization. Now it is time to narrow the focus; it is time to introduce your new volunteers to the jobs they will be doing. The preparation they will need will depend on their job, but there are certain "housekeeping" measures that should be attended to on that first day regardless of their job. The following scenario will give you some idea of how the first day might unfold.

The volunteer manager will introduce the new volunteer to the individual who will be supervising his or her work. If the volunteering contract or agreement has not yet been signed, this should be taken care of now. The supervisor or volunteer manager should review the duties related to the job and confirm the volunteer will be able to carry out those duties. This would also be a good time to review the information in the volunteer's folder to make sure it is current and accurate, particularly the contact information in case of an emergency, and any pertinent information concerning the volunteer's health or physical limitations. If the organization requires a health exam, this should be taken care of at this time.

To make the volunteer more comfortable, the supervisor should provide an informal tour of the work area. The new volunteer should be shown where to find supplies, the closest rest room, the coffee or lunch area, and where he or she can store their purse or  briefcase. The volunteer should be introduced to any staff or other volunteers they will be working with. The supervisor should make sure the volunteer understands what will be expected of him or her in terms of record keeping, and the procedure for the reimbursement of expenses. During the course of this first day the supervisor should encourage feedback to make sure the information presented is being understood and to reassure the volunteer that he or she is being heard.

If the new volunteer is going to be assisting office staff, the initial training will involve such things as acquainting the volunteer with office procedure, explaining office staff responsibilities, introducing the volunteer to the equipment they will be using, and showing him or her how the telephone system works. Because new volunteers are always eager to get to work, if possible, it is a good idea to give your new volunteers a project to do on this first day. If they perform the task well, be affirming. If they have a problem, remind them that this is to be expected during the training period, and reassure them once they become familiar with the work things will go more smoothly.

If the volunteers will be working with clients, or if they have to learn a new skill to do their job, more than one training session probably will be required. If possible, these training sessions should be designed to give the new volunteers a taste of what their job is going to be like so they have a sense, even during training, that they are now an active participant in the work the organization does. Your goal with all new volunteers should be to engage them as quickly as possible so their commitment to your organization can take root and begin to grow.

At the end of that first day the volunteer manager should make a point to visit with the new volunteers briefly to inquire how things went. If any new volunteer expresses any concerns, these should be addressed. Most importantly, the volunteer manager should thank the new volunteers for volunteering and welcome them to the family with the assurance that his or her door will always be open if the new volunteers have any questions or need any help.

Some Tips on Bringing Your Volunteers Onboard

- The personal interview is a key component of the recruitment process and needs to be conducted by a professional, or someone trained and competent in this behavior-based form of interviewing.

- Unlike a job interview, which focuses on filling a job, a volunteer recruitment interview focuses on the potential volunteer and finding a suitable volunteer position for them that suits his or her temperament and will make the best use of his or her talents and skills.

- Using the information the potential volunteer provided in their questionnaire or application, the interviewer crafts open-ended questions for the interview designed to engage the candidate in an informal conversation that will reveal his or her interests, temperament, likes and dislikes, and skills — information the interviewer needs to evaluate the candidate's potential as a volunteer, as well as where this individual would best fit into the organization.

- In addition to the candidate's completed application and a set of prepared open-ended interview questions, the interviewer will bring to the interview detailed information about open volunteer positions and the skills and temperament needed to fill them. The interviewer will also want to provide hand-outs about the organization that the candidates can take with them.

- Volunteer interviews should be held in a pleasant, private, quiet, easily accessible location. You want the room to be cheerful and comfortable, the atmosphere friendly and inviting. By establishing a relaxed, welcoming atmosphere for your interview you will leave your prospective volunteers with the impression they will find volunteering for your organization a pleasant and comfortable experience.

- Volunteer recruitment interviewers need to be part psychologist, part detective, part goodwill ambassador, and part cheerleader as they navigate the complex task of matching a stranger to a volunteer position in a way that benefits both the candidate and the nonprofit.

- Be careful about over-recruiting; you could either end up having to turn down qualified volunteers or accepting individuals for whom you have no work. In either case you could end up creating ill-will.

- One of the questions that should be asked during the personal interview is what the potential volunteer would like to get out of the volunteer experience. Does he or she want to apply existing skills, or is he or she looking to expand their skills by attempting something new? This is a critical consideration when placing the new volunteer.

- For most people, one of the benefits of volunteering is the opportunity it gives them to meet new people who share their interests and values. The social aspect of volunteerism needs to be acknowledged during the orientation process.

- Orientation should do more than inform the new volunteers about the organization, it should inspire enthusiasm and commitment for the nonprofit's mission and work.

- New volunteers come to orientation with the expectation that their volunteer experience is going to change their life in some way. Try to acknowledge this expectation during the orientation program — let them know that you are welcoming them into your volunteer family and have expectations of a new and long-term relationship with them.

- While there are some very important things that need to be accomplished during orientation, this should not be done at the expense of creating an experience that is also fun for the members of the organization and the new volunteers. Humor has a necessary place in this serious ritual.

- Staff, board members, professionals employed by the agency, and volunteers all should take part in welcoming the organization's new volunteers during orientation — both formally and informally.

- Small gestures, such as having someone hand-write and decorate the new volunteer's name tag, personalizes this welcoming ritual and make the new volunteer feel appreciated and welcomed.

- Hold a pre-orientation meeting with your staff, board, and anyone else who will take part in the orientation to discuss the program and to remind them to informally introduce themselves to each of the new volunteers before or after the presentation and thank them for volunteering.

- To draw the new volunteers immediately into a sense of camaraderie, use a buddy system during orientation. Pair the new volunteer with a veteran volunteer to guide him or her through the process and answer any questions.

- By having a veteran volunteer or staff member host two of the new volunteers during the orientation process, you provide the new volunteers with an experienced contact and you give them the opportunity to come away from the orientation with a new friend who shares the common bond of being a newcomer to the organization.

- After the formal presentation, the new volunteers should be given the opportunity to meet with the individual who will be supervising them to solidify what the next steps in their integration into the organizations will be. If all the new volunteers will undergo the same preparation for their work, this can be done at the end of the formal program. If the volunteers will be assuming a diversity of positions requiring different training, each of the supervisors should meet with the volunteers in their charge.

- Another way to show your appreciation for the new volunteers is to have your executive director or volunteer coordinator welcome them individually at the end of the formal presentation.

- Before, after, or as a part of the orientation presentation, time should be set aside to allow each of the new volunteers to stand up, introduce themselves, and provide a brief two- or three-sentence statement about who they are and why they have volunteered.

- It is always a good idea to serve some form of refreshments at an orientation. Having some finger food and beverages available tends to relax people and put them in a good mood.

- One way to effectively communicate that the new volunteers are now accepted and appreciated members of your volunteer team is to provide each one with an official welcoming gift. If they will be required to wear a uniform, as in the case of a hospital or a home building charity, a ceremony can be included to present the volunteers with the jacket or hard hat they will need to wear. In the case of a soup kitchen, the welcoming gift could be an apron. If no uniform is required, it could be a permanent name tag or a parking pass — anything that distinguishes the volunteer from a visitor. It is not the item but the gesture that is important.

- It is a good idea to have a printed program for the orientation that lists not just the details of the program, but also the names of the people in the organization with whom the volunteer will be working, and all the names of the new volunteers. This will serve as a convenient reference for the volunteers and as a keepsake of the event.

- The new volunteers should be sent home with pertinent information about the organization, preferably in the form of the organization's volunteer handbook. This information should include a history of the nonprofit and details about its corporate structure, its mission, and its work. It should also include the names, telephone numbers, and the email addresses of people the volunteer may need to contact.

- To reinforce the positive impact that the orientation hopefully has had on the new volunteer, within two days of the program, the volunteer's supervisor or someone comparable should call the volunteer, thank him or her for attending the orientation, and answer any questions the volunteer might have.

PART TWO:

RETAINING AND MOTIVATING VOLUNTEERS

CHAPTER 7:

IN SEARCH OF LONG-TERM VOLUNTEER COMMITMENT

To keep your volunteers from leaving, you need to understand why they volunteered in the first place. Knowing the answer to this question is the first step in creating a program that encourages long-term volunteer commitment.

Why People Volunteer

According to numerous studies on the subject, an individual usually volunteers for more than one of a wide range of reasons. Here are some of the most frequently mentioned:

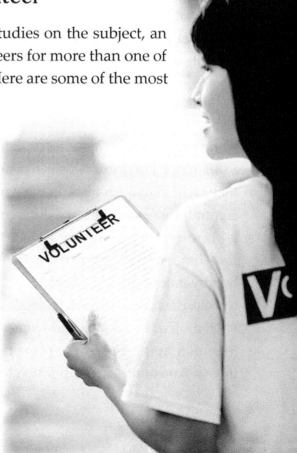

According to a study done in England, volunteering is the second greatest source of individual joy. The first is dancing.

To Feel Good About Themselves

There is something about reaching out to help others that make people feel good. According to Martin Seligman, a professor of psychology at the University of Pennsylvania and a respected proponent of positive psychology, the "highest level of sustained happiness comes when people can give a meaning to their lives." Seligman goes on to say that "Helping others through politics, voluntary work, or religion can help people realize that there is something more important than them." Volunteering is also good for your health. For the past two decades, numerous studies have indicated that volunteering benefits the immune and nervous system and improves life expectancy. A comprehensive review of this research was undertaken by the Corporation for National and Community Service. The report, "The Health Benefits of Volunteering: A Review of Recent Research" can be downloaded at **www.nationalservice.org**.

A Desire to Make a Difference

Almost all the research studies on the subject list this desire to make a difference as a primary reason people volunteer. The difference they want to make may be in the world, in their country, or their community. Sometimes the difference volunteers want to make is in the lives of people they see as less fortunate than themselves; sometimes it is in their own life. This is the motivation that draws hundreds of people to Lutheran Services Florida in times of disaster to help clean up debris, tarp roofs, and cook for survivors. It is what motivates the men and women who volunteer through the Missoula Aging Services to bring meals to the elderly and help them figure out their complicated Medicare claims.

As an Act of Gratitude

These volunteers are frequently individuals who have been affected positively by the work of the organization. They, or someone in their family or circle of friends, may have received direct help. People who volunteer for organizations such as the American Cancer Society or the Alzheimer's Art Quilt Project often do so with the hope that the research they are raising money for will produce results in time to help themselves or someone they care about. Or they may show their appreciation for the work the organization is doing by volunteering in memory of someone whose life the disease has taken.

To Share Their Gifts and Talents

People often volunteer because they want to share their gifts or skills achieved through opportunities that came to them. This is what motivates Dr. Jeffery L. Marsh, a plastic surgeon in St. Louis, whose specialty is an operation that gives babies born with a cleft palate and/or hair lip a chance for a normal life. For one month every fall, he and his wife, Beki, a former operating room nurse, volunteer in Asia where they teach local health care professionals to perform these delicate operations on afflicted individuals from rural communities.

Twelve Reasons People Volunteer

1. To feel good about themselves
2. A desire to make a difference
3. As an act of gratitude
4. To share their gifts and talents
5. To maintain proficiency with an unused skill
6. To acquire new skills and experiences
7. As a way to live their faith
8. To make new friends and build community

9. To realize a sense of accomplishment
10. To help save the world
11. To support and indulge their passion for the arts
12. To follow family tradition

To Maintain Proficiency with an Unused Skill

Individuals who have developed skills in their work life they no longer have an opportunity to use volunteer as a way to maintain proficiency with those skills. A retired accountant, for example, volunteers to help a nonprofit with its finances. A field manager with a large construction company who misses the hands-on work he did early in his career volunteers with his church to build a school in a poor village in Central America.

To Acquire New Skills and Experience

Many young people volunteer to gain experience and build a work history, especially now that corporations and businesses consider volunteering a bona fide work experience. Since the economic downturn, workers who have lost their jobs or who have had their work hours cut back are turning to volunteer work to expand their skills in order to improve their chances of finding a new job.

As a Way to Live Their Faith

Churches, soup kitchens, and organizations that serve the poor and under-served, all draw volunteers motivated by a desire to live their faith. These volunteers may seek long-term service such as volunteering for an ongoing church committee, or they may volunteer routinely to serve holiday dinners to the homeless. Their passion to live their faith may take them abroad, like the chiropractor from Washington State who is currently helping people in an impoverished African community under the sponsorship of her church. Or faith may inspire people to come together for single projects as the parishioners of a Lutheran Church in Washington State did to build a house through Habitat for Humanity.

To Make New Friends and Build Community

The social aspect of volunteering is a major motivator. Many people volunteer to expand their circle of friends, but that is not the only thing they hope to get out of their volunteer experience. They are also seeking acceptance, recognition — all the benefits of being a part of a community. These people hope that by volunteering they will find new friends who will appreciate and value them. They are also motivated by a strong desire to be a part of something bigger than themselves.

To Realize a Sense of Accomplishment

People accomplish things every day in their work life, but if the work is unchallenging, or if they have been doing it so long that it has become routine, they do not feel as if they are accomplishing anything. These people volunteer to find that missing sense of accomplishment. They are looking for that feeling of achievement a volunteer experiences when they help a worthy charity meet a seemingly impossible fundraising goal. They want to know the satisfaction and sense of accomplishment a volunteer feels as they watch a homeless family sit down to a Thanksgiving dinner the volunteer helped to prepare, or when the flawless performance of a church pageant they worked on is applauded and praised.

To Help Save the World

These are the people who put their time and energy into seeking justice, saving the environment, or protecting the vulnerable in our society. They are usually passionate about the causes for which they volunteer and containing that passion is often as much a management issue as retaining their services. These are the volunteers who count birds, save whales, protect children, council rape victims, and fight injustices.

To Support and Indulge Their Passion for the Arts

These are the volunteers who perform, usher, paint scenery, and make costumes in the countless community theaters around the country. They are the volunteers who hand out flyers, sell ads, raise funds, host parties, and provide outreach programs for community orchestras. You will find them working as docents in museums or teaching art in free art clinics for children. Without their volunteers, the country's community theaters and orchestras, museums, and art organizations could not exist. These individuals are driven to volunteer in part by their love of the form of art they support, but they are also seeking social interaction with kindred spirits. They often see themselves as guardians of culture and desire to be recognized and appreciated for the important role they play in perpetuating the arts.

To Follow Family Tradition

There are people for whom volunteering is a way of life — a family tradition. It is something their parents, grandparents, aunts, and uncles have done for as long as they can remember. For them, the idea of not volunteering is unthinkable. Included in this group are those individuals for whom the choice to volunteer, while accepted as a tradition, is really the result of family or peer pressure. Keeping this latter group engaged can prove to be a challenge for a volunteer coordinator.

Becoming clear about what your volunteers want out of their experience with your organization lays the groundwork for creating a volunteer program that encourages long-term commitment. The easiest way to do this is to ask them, but do not expect the real answer on your first try. Chances are the volunteer has not given much thought to the subject. It may take the kind of open-ended, conversation-producing questioning used by your recruitment interviewer to uncover their true expectations. Once you determine what your volunteer expects to get from their volunteer experience, you are ready for the next step: finding a way to create a volunteer experience for that individual that meets his or her expectations.

Circumstances That Affect the Volunteer Experience

Many things affect a volunteer's experience:

- The volunteer's assignment: Does it provide a feeling of purpose and accomplishment?

- The relationship between the volunteer and your staff: Is it good, bad, or indifferent?

- The relationship between the volunteer and other volunteers: Is it harmonious or contentious?

- The environment in which the volunteer works: Is it comfortable, friendly, and inclusive or indifferent and unwelcoming?

- The support — both material and emotional — that the volunteer receives from management: Is the volunteer being given the tools and information he or she needs to do their job?

- The recognition the volunteer is receiving: Is the volunteer feeling appreciated or ignored?

- How well the volunteer feels he or she is being heard: Is anyone requesting or paying attention to the volunteer's input?

- Opportunities for personal growth: Are volunteers pigeonholed with no place to go, or are they provided with opportunities to learn new skills or do new things?

All of these things need to be considered as you build your volunteer program.

Creating Rewarding Volunteer Positions

The effective placement of volunteers is a balancing act. The needs of the organization must be balanced with the needs of the volunteers. The organization's needs are relatively simple: there are certain jobs to be done. The needs of the volunteers are more complex. If your goal as volunteer coordinator is to develop a program that inspires long-term volunteer commitment, you will want to find a way to make those required volunteer positions rewarding for the volunteers who will fill them.

Part of this task has been accomplished by your recruiters who have made every effort to match the skills of the new volunteers to your available volunteer positions. But what works in theory does not always work in practice.

When the Job Is Repetitive or Routine

One of the challenges a volunteer coordinator faces is keeping volunteers happy in positions that are routine and repetitive,

such as supporting office staff. It is a familiar scenario: The recruiting team has found an eager, qualified volunteer willing to fill the position, but after a couple weeks you can see they have become disenchanted. You sense that they are about to head for the door. The job you have placed them in is boring and, on the surface, does not appear to be making any direct contribution to the cause that attracted the volunteer to your organization. The sense of belonging and contribution so necessary to keep a volunteer engaged has never set in.

Sally Wilson coordinates volunteers for Positive Futures Network, the nonprofit organization that publishes *Yes! Magazine*. Retaining volunteers for necessary, but repetitive and mundane, work is a challenge she knows all too well. Here is what she has to say on the subject.

"Engage your volunteers." This mantra is repeated again and again by successful volunteer managers and professional trainers. It applies to all aspects of your volunteer program, but it becomes particularly important when the work you have assigned your volunteer is routine or unchallenging and not obviously connected with your organization's mission: chores such as filing, or stuffing envelopes.

VOLUNTEER STORIES FROM THE FIELD

Yes! Magazine/Positive Futures Network
Bainbridge Island, Washington
Website: **www.yesmagazine.org**

Yes! Magazine is published by the Positive Futures Network, a nonprofit organization based in Bainbridge Island in Washington State. The mission of *Yes!* is to support people worldwide in building a just, sustainable, and compassionate world. The magazine, which is mailed to subscribers throughout the world, is published quarterly. It is produced by a staff of 17, supplemented with interns and volunteers.

Report from: Sally Wilson, fulfillment manager and volunteer coordinator.

For about ten years, when our staff was smaller, I relied on five volunteers, one for each day of the week, to perform certain duties. They came in for two hours on their assigned day to apply postage, prepare checks for banking, take money to the bank and the outgoing mail to the post office, where they picked up our incoming mail. On their return they dated, opened, and distributed the mail around the office and, when the need arose, did various other stuffing, folding, and stamping projects.

Volunteers need to have tasks they can do successfully and feel good about doing. You need to explain what you want them to do simply and clearly, in small enough chunks of information that they are not overwhelmed. You need to take the time to answer questions. Most of all, you need to take the time to talk with them about their lives and what is going on in the organization so they know you care about them, and they have reason to care about the organization. If you just give a volunteer a task and don't engage them, they will not stay. One volunteer told me it was the first time he had a positive experience and felt valued in an office environment. Making sure volunteers feel their service makes a difference and shows that you care about them as people.

One reason your volunteers are there is to feel that they are a part of something. When the job volunteers are given is mundane and does not appear to be related to your organization's mission, they are not going to get the feeling that they are a part of that mission from their assignment. It is your job as volunteer coordinator to help them make that connection — to help them understand that regardless of what they have been given to do, their presence and their effort matters, and they are considered a part of the team. Sally Wilson accomplishes this in the course of a conversation. In a larger organization, her approach should be reinforced by making sure volunteers receive internal communications that update staff on the organization's activities, challenges, and accomplishments. This includes providing your volunteers with copies of your annual reports.

Another way to reinforce your volunteers' sense of being an insider is to provide them with information about upcoming activities before they are announced to the general public. Sally Wilson offers one other suggestion: She invites her volunteers to bring their own brownbag and join the magazine's staff for lunch. This simple act of inclusion reinforces the volunteer's sense of being a part of the organization.

Mixing and Matching Assignments

One way to prevent your volunteer from burning out on a boring job is to mix and match assignments. If your main need for the volunteer is to help with routine office work, perhaps you could expand that volunteer's duties in a way that also utilizes his or her artistic or organizational skills. You might ask her to help make the office more cheerful and inviting by bringing in and arranging fresh flowers from their garden every week. Or you might ask him to keep the bulletin board free from clutter and up-to-date. If she has computer skills, you might assign her the job of designing invitations and fliers for planned events. Maybe you could use him in the office part of the time, and out in the community part of the time, placing posters or delivering fliers. Analyze your needs and your volunteers, and decide if mixing and matching assignments would work for your organization.

Recognizing and Using Talent Effectively

Critical to a volunteer manager's ability to create rewarding volunteer positions is the ability to recognize and effectively utilize volunteer talent. Marisa Albanese is the volunteer coordinator for Union Station Homeless Services in Pasadena, California, an organization that mobilizes large numbers of volunteers on a daily basis. Their volunteers cook and serve breakfast and lunch six days a week at their Adult Center; pick up and stack in-kind donations; perform domestic violence counseling; and work with children in their children's educational and recreational activities. Albanese has a keen eye for spotting and making good use of volunteer talent, as witnessed by this report from the field.

VOLUNTEER STORIES
FROM THE FIELD

Union Station Homeless Services

Pasadena, California

Website: **www.unionstationhs.org**

Union Station Homeless Services operates with a paid staff of 60 and a large, fluctuating support team of volunteers to accomplish their mission of helping men, women, and children in Southern California's San Gabriel Valley rebuild their lives and end homelessness.

Report from Marisa Albanese, Volunteer Coordinator

Last October I had a volunteer who has a strong event planning and organizational background volunteer for a chaotic event. Afterward he wrote me a strongly worded email explaining how the volunteers could have been better organized. I went to the committee for this event and presented his ideas. I even invited him to come to the meeting. Everyone thought his ideas were amazing and we decided to implement them for the next year's event, for which he has agreed to take a more active planning role.

The following month, this man came out for a volunteer day of manual labor before a larger holiday event. Knowing his strength in organization, instead of giving him a manual job, I asked him to gut, organize, and document seven bins we needed for the upcoming large event the following day. He did this better than I could have done myself. I praised him in front of everyone and he committed to coming out to help with this job each time we do the event. Throughout these circumstances, I recognized this man's value and worked to include him on a more strategic level. Before these incidents this man volunteered for us regularly once a month, in addition to helping with special events. Now he is helping us out on a weekly basis. I believe this increase in activity is the result of the appreciation and inclusion he has been given.

According to Marisa Albanese, there are two things every volunteer needs to feel that he or she is a significant part of an organization — two major motivators for volunteering. The first is recognition. The second is being given the opportunity to put his or her talents, skills, and personality to work for the good of the organization. A program that incorporates Albanese's philosophy about volunteers will have a head start in creating an experience that will keep their volunteers coming back.

Some Tips on Laying the Groundwork for Long-Term Volunteer Commitment

- The first step in creating a volunteer program that encourages long-term commitment is to find out what motivated each of your volunteers to volunteer.

- A conversation with your volunteers at the beginning of their service about what prompted their decision accomplishes two things: It provides you with information that will help you keep them engaged and motivated, and it assures them of your interest in helping them to have a rewarding volunteer experience.

- The more you know about your volunteer's interests,

strengths, and talents, the better equipped you will be to place him or her in assignments that will keep them engaged.

- You may not be able to avoid assigning tedious tasks, but with a little imagination you can temper these less desirable assignments with tasks that allow your volunteers to use their creative or organizational skills, such as transforming a dull or disorganized bulletin board into an attractive, organized message center. If the volunteer has computer skills, you might enlist his or her help to design flyers or brochures. By varying your volunteer's assignments in this manner, boring duties become more tolerable.

- Never forget the importance of the social aspect of volunteering. Make it a point to introduce your volunteers to each other and support the friendships that blossom.

- Be sensitive to the discomfort many volunteers feel when they first come into work. Involve them in conversation. Do not assume they know what is going on. Take the time to explain procedures.

- Little things like remembering to use your volunteers' names or asking how their family is show you have taken the time to learn something about them. These simple acts reinforce in the volunteer the feeling that they are important to the organization.

- Your goal is to build a volunteer team. This means creating a sense of camaraderie among new and established volunteers. Arrange for an informal gathering to introduce them to each other. Do not leave the "getting to know each other" to chance. People tend to be shy when thrust among strangers.

Appoint hosts to do the introducing, and prepare them by providing them with information about each individual that might be used to generate conversation. This information might come from volunteer's recruitment application or interview, or personal contact. Does the volunteer being introduced have a special interest, hobby, or talent? Where do he or she work? Where do his or her children go to school?

- When the job you are assigning is routine, take the time to point out its importance to the organization's mission. Even routine office work has a bearing on the organization's ability to carry out its mission.

- Sometimes the pressure generated in fulfilling its mission causes an organization to neglect its environment. New volunteers can be put off or overwhelmed by a stark or cluttered office. This disadvantage can be turned into an advantage. Assigning the new volunteer to help make the office more attractive and inviting can give them a sense of accomplishment and value, while making the office more efficient and comfortable for everyone who works there. However, how you ask your volunteers to do this does matter. Invite them to do this, not as a janitor brought in to clean up after everyone, but as a capable, talented friend whose help would be greatly appreciated.

- After the volunteers have been on the job a couple days, it is a good idea to sit down with them informally and encourage them to talk about their work. While formal evaluations are important, an informal conversation is more likely to draw the volunteer out and expose minor problems. Even little problems can erode a volunteer's enthusiasm and should be attended to.

- In observing your new volunteers on the job, keep an eye out for skills or talents that you will be able to use for future projects. Make a note of these in the volunteer's record. Doing this addresses a number of the motivations that prompt people to volunteer. It communicates recognition and appreciation for the volunteer's skills or talents. This also provides an opportunity for the volunteer to contribute those skills and talents to the nonprofit which, in turn, enables the volunteer to experience a sense of accomplishment.

- When a volunteer appears to be unhappy or is making too many mistakes, sit down and talk with him or her about how they are feeling. If you both agree that the volunteer is not a good fit for the task, try to find a more suitable one. If you cannot find another suitable task for this volunteer, in the process of releasing him or her from the assignment, be sure to let them know you have appreciated their efforts, and thank them for the services they have given you.

- Finding the right task and amount of responsibility for a volunteer requires ongoing monitoring and attention.

- Some volunteers like to work alone on a project; some prefer to work with others. Understanding how your volunteer prefers to work helps you fit him or her to the right job.

- Volunteers bring fresh perspectives and can enrich the office environment. Sometimes they also bring homemade brownies or flowers from their garden.

- People frequently volunteer to achieve a feeling of accomplishment. When this feeling is thwarted by poor planning on the part of the nonprofit or the improper use of the volunteer's time, the volunteer will either scale down his or her activity or quit.

- Many people volunteer in search of personal growth. They want to learn new skills, discover unknown capabilities, learn about themselves and others, or take on new challenges. These desires should be considered when designing volunteer positions.

- Volunteers are not employees. The top-down management model does not work with them. A volunteer supervisor needs a collaborative style; he or she needs to relate to volunteers as equals, not subordinates. The nature of this relationship needs to be established at the beginning of the volunteer's service.

- One way to ease a new volunteer into an organization is to set up a buddy system, pairing an experienced volunteer with a new volunteer for the first couple weeks of the new volunteer's assignment.

- During the beginning of the new volunteer's first assignment, be sure to praise him or her when things go well to reinforce his or her confidence. If mistakes are made, reassure your volunteers that they will learn to do the task in time.

- If the volunteer position is sensitive, stressful, or difficult, it is a good idea to have a probationary period before you make the assignment permanent. This gives you and the volunteer an opportunity to re-evaluate the placement after the volunteer has had some experience with the work.

- According to research, for people to keep volunteering they need to be happy with the supervision and support they are receiving from the non-profit. New volunteers should be encouraged to seek help when needed, and volunteer supervisors and managers need to make asking for help a comfortable experience for their volunteers.

- There are three important things a volunteer coordinator or supervisor needs to accomplish with a new volunteer: (1) Establish criteria for success. (2) Help the new volunteer connect goals to task. (3) Ensure the new volunteer is integrated into the organization and its communication channels.

- Whether dealing with new or well-established volunteers, if a volunteer manager hopes to inspire long-term commitment, he or she needs to develop a management style that acknowledges their volunteers' desire to feel welcome, secure, and respected. Such a style must create the right blend of choice and control, flexibility and organization, and informality and efficiency.

CHAPTER 8:

VOLUNTEERS AND STAFF RELATIONS

The desire to volunteer may be innate, but how an individual chooses to fulfill that desire is a matter of choice. Because qualified volunteers are essential to your ability to fulfill your mission, you have done your best to persuade people to express their need to be of service by volunteering for your organization.

So far, your efforts have paid off. Your successful recruitment campaign has yielded a fresh crop of promising volunteers, and your carefully planned orientation appears to have reinforced their enthusiasm for your work and mission. Initial training has been completed and you have finally brought your new volunteers onboard. The question now is will you be able to keep them onboard? This will depend on the kind of volunteer experience they have with your organization.

The Critical Role of Staff in Volunteer Retention

A hostile or uncooperative staff can thwart a nonprofit's best efforts to provide a satisfying volunteer experience. This is not to imply that the staff intentionally sets out to sabotage the volunteer program, but sometimes concerns or attitudes get in the way of their ability to deal constructively with volunteers. This is why volunteer management consultants stress the importance of taking the time to prepare your staff before you bring new volunteers onboard.

Hopefully you have heeded this advice. You have involved your staff in your recruiting efforts and you have welcomed and heeded their input in designing your new volunteer positions. You have also made a strong case for the value these new volunteers will bring to the organization and pointed out specifically how they will benefit the staff. Sometimes, however, even with this preparation, the issue persists. Let us take a look at some of the concerns that trigger an anti-volunteer attitude. According to the research, some staff members resist working with volunteers because:

• Volunteers make mistakes

• Volunteers lack adequate training

• They fear that the volunteers will spy on them and report them to administrative personnel

• Training volunteers takes too much time — it is easier to do the task themselves

• Volunteers constantly distract staff with questions

• Volunteers give staff no privacy

• The volunteer will learn the job and replace the staff member

Some of these objections are based on fear or insecurity, but some are legitimate. Volunteers do make mistakes; they are frequently untrained and their numerous questions can distract employees from their work. Having volunteers around the office does infringe on the staff's sense of privacy, and there is no doubt that it is often quicker and easier for the employee to do the job themselves than take the time to show a volunteer how to do it. Whether your employees' objections are irrational and born out insecurity, or have a legitimate basis, they need to be addressed if you want to establish good volunteer-staff relations.

Policy Relationships:
Corporate Section Number 5.0
Human Resources Sub-section
Number: 5.11
Effective Date: July 2004

VANCOUVER ISLAND
healthauthority

Volunteer services are often conducted in close proximity to paid staff. Therefore, good relations between volunteers and staff are necessary. The goal for which we strive is an atmosphere in which staff welcomes volunteers, understand their role and do not feel their livelihood threatened by them, and in which volunteers understand the boundaries of their role and feel accepted by staff as a part of the health care team.

The use of volunteer resources shall be supernumerary to established staff positions and the involvement of volunteers shall not result in the layoff of any employee; nor shall volunteers be used to fill positions that are filled by paid staff on either a regular, part-time or casual basis.

Addressing Staff Fears

Clarity of roles is essential in creating a good relationship between employees and volunteers. The duties and rights of each should be clearly defined and documented. The most effective documents are created with input from staff and experienced volunteers.

A good way to ease your employees' concern about volunteers learning their job and replacing them is to have an established organization policy that clearly states you recruit volunteers to supplement, not supplant, staff. For an example of the kind of wording you might use in preparing your policy statement, refer to the accompanying sample provided by the Vancouver Island Health Authority. You can view the entire document on the website listed in the bibliography.

In presenting this policy to your employees, it helps if you can cast their role as that of a manager or mentor — someone who is charged with guiding volunteers through their learning experience. You might also want to stress how working with volunteers provides an opportunity for your staff to develop their managerial skills, which will strengthen their résumé and open opportunities for future advancement. In other words, you want your staff to make a positive connection between the success of your volunteer program and their own personal goals.

The idea that volunteers might spy on them comes from the employee's conflicted perception that volunteers are outsiders not to be trusted, and at the same time, because they are catered to by administration, enjoy a favored relationship with management. This perception can best be addressed by strengthening the relationship between that employee and your volunteers. One way to accomplish this is to encourage your volunteers to reach out to the staff. You might suggest, for example, that they:

- Throw a surprise party for the staff to thank them for their help

- Bring in homemade cookies to share on coffee breaks

- Send birthday cards to the staff — you provide the dates

- Invite the staff and their families to a barbeque or picnic so your volunteers and staff can get to know each other better

In encouraging a closer relationship between your staff and your volunteers you are again faced with a balancing act. You need to reassure your staff that volunteers pose no threat to their job security. At the same time, you also need to make it clear to them that staff and volunteer contributions and time are valued equally by your organization. Unless your staff and volunteers both recognize they are respected and valued equally, they will not be able to work together in harmony.

Stressing Value Over Burden

Let us assume that during the recruitment process you successfully made the case to your staff that volunteers would benefit their department. Your employees reacted positively to the idea of getting help with their workload. But now that your volunteers are on site and your staff is seeing the amount of time they require, your employees are beginning to feel that the cost outweighs the benefits. How do you convince them otherwise?

Marisa Albanese, volunteer coordinator for Union Station Homeless Services, uses discernible evidence of her volunteers' contributions to make the point.

 # VOLUNTEER STORIES
FROM THE FIELD

 Union Station Homeless Services
Pasadena, California
Website: **www.Unionstationhs.org**

Union Station's administrative office supports a large, complex outreach program. It is the second main area, after their adult center kitchen, in which volunteers are used. They use volunteers for clerical work, database entry, reception work, filling, mailing — anything and everything staff members may need.

Report from Marisa Albanese, volunteer coordinator

One of the greatest challenges I have faced as Volunteer Coordinator has been to get staff members onboard with the great potential that lies in volunteer programming. Although I have worked to train staff on how to interact with volunteers, they often see utilizing volunteer support as more work than help. It is super difficult to get staff to think outside of the box of what needs volunteers can or cannot fill. Even though I know a need exists and a volunteer could work to fill the gap, staff members find it difficult to think through managing and training a volunteer to help out. Similarly, it is a challenge to get staff members to really take ownership of managing their volunteers.

As I work to train staff for volunteer management I strive to emphasize the worth of volunteers and to get them excited about utilizing volunteers. One of the ways that I feel I have made some progress in this area is by developing a volunteer hour tracking system. I have encouraged them to not only report volunteer hours to me, but to keep a record of the hours volunteers fill in their department for their own reporting board.

Marisa Albanese employs a two-tier approach to demonstrate volunteer value. Instead of having volunteers record their hours directly with her, Albanese involves the staff in the process. This makes them more conscious of the significant number of hours volunteers are contributing to their department. Albanese then reinforces this awareness by also having the staff record volunteer hours on their record board.

Here is another suggestion that enables you to demonstrate volunteer value while honoring the burden volunteers place on employees: have your employees keep a record of the time they spend training volunteers. Eventually there will come a point when the volunteers' productive hours will outnumber the hours the staff must invest in training them. Have the employees look for and note that point. Making them aware of their volunteers' transition from encumbrance to asset can cause a positive adjustment in their attitude toward their volunteers.

Another way to temper negative feelings an employee might have about volunteers is to place your most efficient volunteer with the negative employee to give him or her the best possible experience with a volunteer. Or to ease the burden on that employee, you might assign an experienced volunteer to supervise your new volunteer — in cooperation with the employee — until the new volunteer is ready to work on their own.

The Issue of Privacy

New volunteers are in a learning mode and filled with uncertainty and questions. Your employees have their workloads to attend to and they are probably working in an environment that makes volunteer access to them relatively easy. It is understandable that some of them may feel overburdened by the neediness of your volunteers. If they have no way to escape, they are going to feel resentful. They need privacy — some time free from volunteer contact. Here are some ideas that have worked for others:

- Arrange volunteer hours so when your employees come to work they will have the first hour to themselves to catch up on work or enjoy coffee and conversation with each other before the volunteers come in.

- Arrange a spot in your office modeled after a teacher's lounge where volunteers are not allowed entrance. Your employees can go there for coffee breaks, to eat lunch, or just to get away for a few minutes from the stress of their job.

- Create some desk signs your employees can use to alert volunteers not to disturb them when an assignment they are working on requires concentration.

Management's Role in Promoting Good Staff-Volunteer Relations

Your staff has been paying attention to how your CEO or executive director and your board of directors relate to your volunteer program. All your efforts to create a good volunteer-staff relationship will be to no avail if your staff has not received the message that your volunteer program has the complete support of management. Without this declared support, your volunteer program will have no credibility with your employees.

Did your CEO or executive director play a prominent role in welcoming your new volunteers? What about your board? Even though board positions in most nonprofits are volunteer positions, often the structure of the organization creates a wall between these volunteers and volunteers who work with staff or clients. Board volunteers are viewed differently by staff than support volunteers. Have you done anything to impress upon your staff the commitment your management has made to your

volunteer program? Has their support been publicized in your in-house publications? Has your CEO or executive director spoken to your employees directly about their commitment to your volunteer program? Before you can ask your staff to support your volunteer program, you need to make sure they know that the policymakers and implementers in your organization support it.

Be Willing to Make Adjustments

No plan is perfect. You may have designed a good program for utilizing your new volunteers. The recruiters may have found a volunteer who appears to be perfect for an assignment. But what works on paper does not always work as smoothly in practice. There may be an unpredicted clash of temperament between a staff member and a volunteer, or between two volunteers assigned to work together. Or the job conceived may turn out to be different than the job in practice, making the volunteer less suitable for the position. It is important that you re-evaluate your volunteer assignments on a regular basis.

This evaluation procedure should begin within the first two weeks of placement, and should be based on feedback from both the volunteer and the staff members involved in the assignment. If either the volunteer or the staff perceives a serious problem — one that cannot be settled amicably by some minor adjustments — you need to address that problem as quickly as possible.

Handling Staff-Volunteer Conflict

Even in the best-run volunteer programs, conflicts can arise between staff and volunteers. Ameliorating these conflicts is not a simple matter of determining who is right and who is wrong; the issues are more complex.

For argument's sake, let us say the employee is clearly at fault. In the for-profit world, one option the manager would have would be to fire that employee. In the nonprofit world, such action could create irreparable damage to both employee morale and the volunteer program.

The volunteer manager faces a similar dilemma if the volunteer is the cause of the problem. Volunteers cannot simply be dismissed; an effort must be made to reassign the individual if possible, an action that involves its own set of challenges. The exception would be if the conflict was triggered by a breach of appropriate conduct on the part of the volunteer, as defined by the organization's policies. (The procedure for firing a volunteer will be discussed in Chapter 12.)

The volatile nature of volunteer-employee conflicts is why mediation skills are considered an essential qualification for a volunteer manager. Mediation is the only viable approach to handling volunteer-employee conflicts.

Tips for Mediating Volunteer-Employee Conflicts

- Meet jointly with the volunteer and the employee.

- Clarify your role as an impartial mediator.

- Have each party summarize their perspective of the situation without interruption.

- Restate your understanding of the problem and ask them to confirm that your assessment is correct.

- Ask the two parties to work out and agree to a mutually acceptable solution to the problem.

When conducting mediation, it is essential to meet with both parties at the same time to prevent them from becoming polarized in their positions. Before you begin you should make it clear you are impartial and that the purpose of the meeting is not to place blame but to resolve the issue.

The volunteer and the employee should each be given a chance to tell their side of the story without interruption from you or the other party. After they have both presented their perspective on the situation, restate your understanding of the problem and ask them to confirm your interpretation. Once agreement is reached on what the problem is, ask both parties what action they would like to see the other person take to resolve the situation. It is important that you keep this conversation focused on solutions, not personalities.

The final step in the process is to have your employee and your volunteer work out and agree on what action needs to be taken to solve the problem. Assure both parties you have every faith in their ability to resolve the issue and thank them for their efforts.

When a Solution Cannot Be Reached

If the situation cannot be corrected with mediation, the volunteer coordinator must try to find the volunteer another suitable assignment. Dealing with the employee is a more complex problem. Another, hopefully more compatible, volunteer may be found to assist them, or the volunteer coordinator may conclude that the appropriate action would be to provide no further volunteer help for this employee. The decision should be based on which choice would be best for the department and the volunteer program.

When Clients Are Involved

Conflicts can also occur in situations where volunteers are assisting staff in outreach programs that involve clients. If the clients are children, the elderly, or any other vulnerable population, the first consideration in dealing with a staff-volunteer conflict must be the welfare and safety of the organization's clients.

Fortunately, staff that work with volunteers in these programs usually have a strong appreciation of the volunteers' contributions, and the volunteers usually have great respect for the professional staff they assist. The conflicts that do arise are frequently triggered by stress or a misunderstanding, and can often be resolved by better communication or additional training for the volunteers and/or the professional staff.

A Few More Thoughts About Volunteer-Staff Relations

Volunteers cannot be forced on staff. Your staff must be adequately prepared to accept them, but your job does not end there. To maintain a harmonious relationship between your staff and your volunteers, you need to remind your staff frequently of the value of volunteers, preferably by pointing out specific examples of how the volunteers are helping to ease staff workload.

How you place your volunteers also affects your staff's attitude toward them. If your placements are done haphazardly, your staff will not see your volunteers as relevant to their job and will

view them as a burden rather than a help. This attitude will be reflected in the way they treat your volunteers, causing your volunteers to feel unappreciated and unwanted — not feelings conducive to making a long-term commitment to your organization.

Some Tips on Creating and Maintaining Good Volunteer-Staff Relations

- The first step in creating a harmonious relationship between your staff and your volunteers is to define and document their roles.

- Do not rely on a job description for defining staff roles; they are only a suggestion of what the job might be. Have your employees provide a comprehensive list of all their duties and responsibilities. The volunteer's job description should be compiled by the volunteer coordinator in concert with the employees the volunteer will be assisting and the volunteer.

- To defuse fears that volunteers will take jobs away from staff, establish a documented policy that ensures your organization will not replace full-time or part-time staff with volunteers. (See sample wording from the Vancouver Island Health Authority in this chapter.)

- The best way to convince your staff that volunteers are more of a benefit than a burden is to provide concrete proof of this. Under the pressure of doing their job, your staff may not notice the productive hours your volunteers are contributing to ease their workload. Keep pointing this out, verbally and through your in-house publications.

- Institute an award for the employee who has been most valuable to the volunteers. It could be a plaque, a certificate they can frame, a custom coffee cup, or something specific to your organization. Have your volunteers hold a ceremony to present the award. This could be done monthly, every six months, or once a year. Include a personal thank you from a volunteer representative.

- Encourage volunteers to perform impromptu gestures to show their appreciation for the staff they work with by bringing in fresh flowers or plants from their garden, baking cookies for them, or bringing in cards on their birthdays or special anniversaries.

- Encourage volunteers to have seasonal parties — picnics, barbecues, holiday parties —and invite the staff and their families so staff and volunteers can get know each other better.

- In placing your volunteers, if you notice in their records that they share any common interests with the employees they will be working with, take the time to help the volunteer and staff member make that connection. For example, if they both like to knit, are interested in a particular sport, or both have grandchildren, bring it to their attention. Such connections take away that sense of "other" that often triggers distrust and makes it difficult for people to relate to each other.

- Encourage your staff to welcome volunteers to join them for lunch occasionally. It could be a brownbag affair or a quick trip to a neighborhood restaurant. They may do it initially as a concession to make the volunteer feel more comfortable, but the more time your employee spends with your volunteer in a social setting, the more comfortable they will be in working with them.

- If you sense tension developing in a volunteer-staff situation, take preventative action. Get the staff together when the volunteers are not around and without targeting specifics, explore what their general feelings are about whether the volunteer help is working out. Discuss what they think is working, what they think is not working, and invite them to offer solutions on how to make the program more efficient. Do not just listen; implement any measures that might help the situation, and credit the individual who came up with the idea.

- If you have an employee who is reluctant to work with volunteers, assign one of your best volunteers to work with that individual — someone who is pleasant, capable, and efficient. Let the volunteer do the evangelizing for you.

- The best way to deal with a capable employee who is hostile to volunteers may be by not providing one for him or her. At the very least you will not have to deal with any conflicts his or her hostility would cause. At best, when they realize that the volunteers are actually making work easier for some of their co-workers, they might change their attitude and request one.

- Perception is often the cause of anti-volunteer feelings among staff. If you recast the employee's perception of their role in the relationship you might be able to recast their attitude toward the volunteer. If the employee sees himself or herself as managing or mentoring the volunteer, the time they must spend teaching them the job might be more palatable.

- You want your staff to have a vested interest in seeing your volunteer program succeed. For that to happen they must feel they profit in some way from the program. The help they receive may not be perceived as reason enough, but if they recognize that the management aspect of their work with volunteers is building their management skills and strengthening their résumé they might view the time they must spend teaching volunteers as an investment instead of a burden. It is up to you, as volunteer coordinator, to point this out to them.

- When conflict between staff and volunteers cannot be avoided, mediation is the only viable way to handle the situation.

- One way to demonstrate the effectiveness of volunteers is to publish your success stories periodically in your in-house or external newsletter or on your website. Instead of following the traditional path of spotlighting the volunteer, feature a dynamic relationship between a volunteer and a staff member, with quotes from the staff member about the tremendous help the volunteer has provided. This testimonial can also be used as a recruiting tool.

- Have your staff nominate candidates for the most valuable volunteer of the month by submitting a paragraph explaining their nomination. Have the staff member who nominated the winner present the award at a formal or informal ceremony. In presenting the award the employee should specify why he or she nominated the volunteer, and thank the volunteer for the valuable help they have provided. This exercise makes everyone think about the value of the volunteers they work with.

- To prevent stress over staff involvement with volunteers make sure you and the staff are in agreement over who is in charge of what regarding each volunteer. A clear understanding of responsibilities will avoid confusion and resentment.

- For good staff-volunteer relations, it is important that volunteers understand the needs and concerns of the staff and respect the boundaries defined by their volunteer assignment.

- Your staff needs and deserves some privacy. It is important that they have either protected time or space that allows them relief from exposure to the needs and demands of volunteers.

- Do not wait for problems to occur to solicit employee feedback on your volunteer placements. Ask for that feedback periodically. Even if things are going smoothly, this will remind your employees you are concerned about the impact of the program on them.

- Your attitude in discussing and dealing with volunteer issues will affect how your staff perceives the program. If you approach your discussions as though you are expecting problems, you will probably find them. If you are upbeat and project the attitude that this is a program that can only benefit the organization and your staff, most of the time your staff will approach the program with that same expectation.

- Always be aware that a conflict between an employee and a volunteer affects more than the two parties directly involved. The conflict poisons the work environment, affecting other relationships and interfering with the staff's ability to get work done. Never ignore a budding conflict in the hope it will solve itself. Resolve it quickly.

- An occasional volunteer-staff conflict is to be expected, but if there are a rash of conflicts — even small ones — it is time to take a hard look at the work environment to see if something there is triggering the situation.

- Follow the advice given by volunteer consultants Rick Lynch and Steve McCurley: Think of the volunteer-staff relationship as a triangular relationship involving staff, volunteers, and the volunteer manager. As volunteer manager, your role is to keep the other two sides of this triangle — the staff and the volunteer — balanced.

CHAPTER 9:

CREATING A VOLUNTEER-FRIENDLY ENVIRONMENT

While an attractive, comfortable facility can give a nonprofit the appearance of being volunteer friendly, the nonprofit will not be able to successfully create a true volunteer friendly environment unless the desire to create it is deeply rooted in the organization's culture. An organization's culture, according to Edgar Schein, Sloan Fellows professor of management emeritus and a prominent theorist of organizational culture, is "a pattern of shared basic assumptions that a group learned as it solved its problems of external adaptation and internal integration, that has worked well enough to be considered valid and, therefore, to be taught to new members as the correct way you perceive, think, and feel in relation to those problems." From the organization's point of view, it is simply "the way we do things around here."

Whether developed consciously or unconsciously, every organization has a culture — a specific way it perceives and pursues its mission; a management style that determines how its staff interacts, or deals with clients or volunteers. "The bottom line for leaders," Schein says, "is that if they do not become conscious of the culture in which they are embedded, those cultures will manage them."

For some clues to what creates this sense of culture, we must again refer to why people volunteer. Two motivations most frequently mentioned are a desire for social interaction and a wish to be a part of some greater cause — some effort they perceive to be of value. But before we discuss how these expectations relate to making your volunteers comfortable, let us take a moment to consider a less complex component of a volunteer-friendly environment — a nonprofit's physical space.

It is easy for smaller nonprofits with a limited paid staff to get so caught up in the pressures of pursuing their mission that they lose sight of the role their physical surroundings play in helping them retain volunteers. The relationship of space to retaining volunteers for larger, successful nonprofits brings up a different set of issues. Let us begin with the smaller nonprofits first.

The Role of the Physical Environment in Retaining Volunteers

An organization's mission may attract volunteers, but if the workspace the nonprofit provides for those volunteers is allowed to fall into disrepair, the possibility of them making a long-term commitment will decrease. Aside from being uncomfortable to work in, shabbiness, clutter, and neglect do little to inspire confidence in an organization's ability to carry out its mission.

What is required here is a little imagination, ingenuity, and, at most, a small outlay of cash. Some or all of the costs involved can be coved with donations and in-kind services. To transform an uninviting space into a pleasant, comfortable environment for your volunteers and staff, you can begin by adding a little color.

While giving decorating advice is beyond the scope of this book, a brief discussion of the power of color will hopefully inspire you to take a fresh look at your workspace with an eye toward making it more serviceable and inviting for your volunteers and staff.

Color has the remarkable ability to transform a space and change the impact it has on people. A blue or green room tends to make people feel at peace. Pink and lavender shades remind people of love, and spaces that are predominantly purple project a regal or noble feeling. Interestingly enough, color also contributes to how a person perceives the temperature, humidity, and even the smell of a place. The color orange, for example, tends to make people feel warmer and dryer, while a room that is predominantly blue or green tends to make them feel cooler and perceive the space as having a clean, fresh aroma.

What kind of environment do you want to create? Is your mission stressful? Do you want to make your environment more peaceful? Is trash and grime a problem in your neighborhood? Do you want your offices to feel clean? Pick the colors that will help you establish the feeling you want for your space, the kind of environment that will make your staff and volunteers more comfortable and productive. Then, with a few cans of paint and some volunteer manpower, begin your transformation. Add a few pieces of spruced-up second hand furniture and a potted plant or two and you have a fresh, inviting space everyone can feel at home in — a space in which volunteers will enjoy spending their time.

Sending the Right Message with Your Physical Space

Usually the ability to create an attractive, comfortable environment for your volunteers and clients is a good thing. But sometimes it can be too much of a good thing. Take, for example, the situation that confronted the Santa Fe Rape Crisis & Trauma Treatment Center in New Mexico several years ago when the organization finally raised enough money to build its own facility.

Appreciative of the therapeutic value of beauty, SFRC & TTC's executive director, Barbara Goldman, and her staff wanted their new home to be more than functional. They wanted to create a beautiful and comforting environment for the treatment of their clientele of severely traumatized young children and adults. Over the years, the agency has attracted the support of many talented local artists who offered to help. Some valuable pieces of art were donated to embellish the new building. The gifts were deeply appreciated, but they created the possibility of a perception problem for the organization.

SFRC & TTC's executive director and board became concerned that the expensive collection of art was sending the wrong message to the community, and especially to potential volunteers and donors, whom they feared might see the art as an indication of misdirected resources. To prevent this misconception, they decided to be proactive. They publicized the gifts, giving credit to the donors. On-site they clearly credited each piece of art as a donation. Through these actions, SFRC & TTC managed to circumvent any misunderstandings about the gifts.

A successful brand is crucial to a nonprofit's ability to fulfill its mission and attract and keep volunteers. Having an attractive, tasteful, professional looking office or facility plays an important role in creating and sustaining a strong brand. But the line between tasteful and opulent can sometimes become blurred in the eyes of supporters who may mistake the organization's expression of good taste as a sign of poor stewardship. It is an issue of perception, but important nonetheless, and nonprofits need to be alert to this possibility when they build or remodel their facilities.

Creating a Welcoming, Friendly Organizational Culture

A nonprofit's physical environment contributes to its ability to provide a volunteer-friendly environment, but the nonprofit will not be able to successfully create that environment unless the desire to create it is deeply rooted in the organization's culture. Here is a brief quiz to help you evaluate how deeply embedded the idea of volunteer-friendliness is in the culture of your organization:

1. When a volunteer or guest enters your facility, are they:

    a. Acknowledged immediately with a friendly smile?

    b. Acknowledged immediately in a business-like manner?

    c. Ignored until they press the issue?

2. When a volunteer or visitor enters a work area, does:

    a. A member of your staff get up and greet them?

    b. Your staff acknowledge them with a smile?

    c. Your staff remain focused on their work until approached?

3. When showing a volunteer or guest around, does the staff member:

    a. Make an effort to introduce the guest or volunteer to everyone by name?

    b. Only introduce the guest or volunteer to people who come up to them?

    c. Make no introductions?

4. On breaks, are volunteers:

    a. Invited to join your staff?

    b. Directed to facilities?

    c. Ignored?

5. During gatherings, does your staff:

    a. Involve your volunteers in conversations?

    b. Remain in their own cliques, but treat the volunteers politely when approached?

    c. Ignore the volunteers?

If you answered "a" to all the questions, your organization is on the right track. If you answered "b" you have some work to do. If you answered "c" you have a great deal of work to do.

While these questions focused on staff behavior, staff behavior is always a reflection of the organization's culture. Management may hold volunteers in high esteem. They may even recognize that every guest is a potential supporter and should be treated graciously. But if staff behavior reflects indifference or rudeness, obviously management has failed to communicate their philosophy about volunteers to their employees.

Let us clarify that we are not talking about an isolated incident or a problem with one employee, such as a receptionist who needs better training in his or her position. These situations can be addressed one-on-one in private meetings. What we are concerned with here is a systemic problem throughout an organization. If volunteer retention is a serious goal, then establishing a consistent, constructive philosophy throughout your organization regarding the treatment of volunteers is essential. To do this will require investing some time and effort in helping your staff improve their skills in dealing with people.

"Civility: Civilized conduct, especially courtesy, politeness. A polite act or expression."

— Merriam-Webster's 11th Collegiate Dictionary

Give Your Employees a Reason to Care

Your employees' unresponsive or inconsiderate attitude toward volunteers is probably not intentional. They simply have found no reason to behave differently. The first thing you need to do to change their behavior is provide them with a reason to change their behavior. They may even have gotten your message that volunteers are important to the organization, but still not connected that message to their specific relationship with the volunteers. You need to help them make that connection. To succeed, any program you set up to reshape your staff's behavior toward volunteers must begin with giving them a compelling reason to change their current behavior. Here are some motivations you might consider:

- Include the ability to work well with volunteers as a critical component of your employee's job description.

- Stress the relationship of retaining volunteers to your organization's ability to function, and relate this to your employees' job security.

- Connect an employee's value to his or her ability to create good will for the organization through their relationship with volunteers.

- Establish a reward-producing competition among employees based on who does the most to create a strong relationship between your organization and your volunteers.

Creating a Volunteer-Friendly Staff

One of the most effective ways to bring about a change in your staff's attitudes and behavior toward volunteers is to set up an organization-wide training program to teach everyone basic relationship-building skills. You can bring in a professional trainer or you can create your own program in-house using resources from professional associations or the internet. A list of these resources can be found in the resource section of this book. Here are some subjects you may want to cover in your retraining program:

- The appropriate way to greet people
- Developing good listening skills
- Understanding body language
- How to defuse difficult situations using tact
- Simple rules of courtesy
- The "doing unto others" principle

What we are really discussing here is a course in civility. While today's hectic society does not promote civility, because nonprofits depend on the good will of the public, the idea and practice of civility needs to be an integral part of their culture. Management needs to model it in its treatment of staff; staff needs to be encouraged to practice it in their dealings with clients and volunteers. Civility is at the very core of a volunteer-friendly environment. So is gratitude.

Building a Culture of Gratitude

The idea that it is important to thank volunteers is not new; volumes have been written on the subject. Lists of traditional or creative new ways to say thank you can be found in books and on the internet. But gratitude should not be just a gesture an organization indulges in occasionally to try to show they care, nor should it be viewed as a carrot to keep volunteers involved. For a nonprofit serious about retaining its volunteers, gratitude needs to be a mind-set, a deliberate style of doing business; it needs to be an integral part of the organization's culture so the practice of gratitude becomes second nature for its employees.

Gratitude must be stressed in employee training. The receptionist must be instructed that his or her primary job is not to answer phones, but to make whoever walks through your door feel comfortable and at ease, because your organization is grateful for their interest and support. Your office staff must be made to understand that beyond the job they have been hired to do, they are expected to demonstrate the organization's gratitude to volunteers, donors, and prospective donors by being courteous and helpful.

Gratitude should not be saved for award banquets and appreciation luncheons. In an organization that fosters a culture of gratitude, instead of being viewed as a calculated strategy to keep volunteers happy, saying thank you for even the smallest effort or accomplishment becomes second nature — a truly spontaneous expression of appreciation. In such a culture, personalizing expressions of gratitude is no longer a challenge because people learn to appreciate each other and instinctively know how to express their gratitude in a personal way.

A culture of civility and gratitude creates an environment where volunteers feel welcome and appreciated, and an organization they are proud to be a part of. But there is still the issue of social interaction.

Getting Your Employees to Engage Volunteers

People volunteer out of a desire for social interaction. This expectation is met in part by their relationship with other volunteers, but your staff also has a part to play in meeting that expectation. As Marisa Albanese explains, for an organization to be volunteer-friendly, volunteers need to feel that they are seen by that organization as people, not just extra help.

VOLUNTEER STORIES FROM THE FIELD

Union Station Homeless Services

Pasadena, California

Website: **www.unionstationhs.org**

Union Station Homeless Services, an agency with a reputation for being volunteer-friendly, has a paid staff of 60 employees.

Report from Marisa Albanese, volunteer coordinator

Many people volunteer because they want social interaction. I feel that a large mistake that is often made with administrative volunteers is staff members can easily make the mistake of treating volunteers as they would other staff members.

When training staff to work with volunteers I always remind them that a large reason why volunteers choose to give their time freely is because they want to feel a part of something bigger and they want to have some kind of social interaction. Administrative staff frequently forget this, leaving volunteers to do data entry or filing for hours at a time without ever checking in with them. I ask staff to not leave a volunteer alone for more than 25 minutes at a time without checking in on them. This way, staff members feel a connection to the often mundane work the volunteer is doing.

In the same way, I encourage staff members to reserve the first five minutes of a volunteer's shift to just chatting. Staff members should show a genuine interest in the lives of their volunteers, making it fun for a volunteer to work with that person.

There is no great mystery to creating a volunteer-friendly environment. Just think of your volunteers as important guests coming for a visit. You know they are coming, so you make your home as attractive and welcoming as you can. When they arrive, you treat them with civility. You introduce them to everyone, and include them in conversations and activities. To show your hospitality, you offer them refreshments. Because these are special guests whom you would like to see again, you do everything you can to make their visit a pleasurable one.

Your volunteers should be treated in the same manner. And they will be, automatically, if you establish a culture for your organization that prizes civility and gratitude; a culture that views every volunteer as a welcome guest whom everyone appreciates and wants to return again and again. Accomplish this and you will have created a volunteer-friendly environment — the kind of environment that encourages long-term volunteer commitment.

Some Tips On Creating a Volunteer-Friendly Environment

- Review your volunteer workspace to make sure it is volunteer-friendly. Is it clean, uncluttered, a place you would like to spend time if you did not have to be there? Are there some inexpensive things you can do to make it more welcoming?

- How do you rate the level of civility in your nonprofit's culture? Is it being modeled by management and practiced by employees?

- Try this conscious-raising exercise with your staff during one of your staff meetings: Ask them to talk about what bothers them most when they shop in a retail establishment. As they begin to talk about the lack of attention they get from store employees (and they will), draw them out about how they feel when this happens. Does it make them feel frustrated, angry? Then make the connection for them with the way volunteers may feel when the staff is too busy to acknowledge them. Ask them how to fix the problem.

- Set up some role playing situations to teach the proper way to greet people. Have staff members take turns playing the volunteer. Create scripts for them. Make it fun: have some of the scripts exaggerate the conversations just for laughs to loosen the group up. Greeting is more than words. Stress the importance of body language, looking the person in the eyes, and smiling. Encourage them to apply what they learn after the session. Compliment your employees when you observe them applying what they have learned in their dealings with each other or volunteers.

- Meet with volunteers and give them an opportunity to tell you what they think would make them more comfortable in their work with your organization. Implement all feasible suggestions. The next month, have a follow-up meeting to see if they noticed the changes and if the changes made any difference for them.

- Observe your receptionist for a few days without calling attention to what you are doing. Make some notes about what you believe she or he is doing well, and where you think she or he can improve. Also ask some of the volunteers your receptionist comes in contact with about their reaction to the interaction they have with the receptionist. Prepare some suggestions on how your receptionist could better advance your goal of becoming a more volunteer-friendly organization. Meet with the receptionist. Be sure to start the meeting by complimenting him or her for all the things they do well. Give him or her a list of changes you would like to implement and explain the reason for each one. Follow up in a month using the same process. If the performance you observe has no redeeming qualities, replace your receptionist with someone who can be volunteer-friendly. It is too important a spot to fill carelessly.

- If your volunteers bring in homemade treats occasionally, ask your employees to do the same. It is a subtle way of putting employees and staff on the same plane, and also suggests that your employees like your volunteers enough to treat them.

- Put up a chalkboard where volunteers can write messages — a slate Twitter station. Encourage staff and volunteers to post messages about things that are going on in their lives that they would like to share: new children or grandchildren, awards they have received outside of the organization, causes they want to promote, a good joke they heard, or a movie or piece of music they want to recommend. Determine a policy for how long an announcement can stay on the board and require each note be dated. Put someone in charge of erasing a note after a certain length of time.

- Give staff a list of volunteers' birthdays and suggest that they send cards to those volunteers they work with most.

- Encourage your staff to send or give thank you notes to volunteers when they do something for them beyond their assigned task. This can include bringing in occasional cookies, or helping out with duties not assigned to them when the employee is under pressure to get something done.

- If civility is not intrinsic in your organization, hold a meeting and after an explanation of what civility is, have your staff discuss what your organization would look like if the rule of civility would be required in their contact with each other and with volunteers. What kind of difference would it make on the stress level everyone works under, on the issue of volunteer-staff relations? Try the same idea with the practice of gratitude.

- Have a smile day once a month with the mandate that for that day everyone — employee or volunteer — will be required to smile every time they request something, or give someone something. Laughing will be allowed, but smiling will be required.

- Put a jigsaw puzzle in the lunchroom or coffee area and invite staff and volunteers to add a couple pieces at lunch and on break. Mark the completion with a mini-ceremony to celebrate the teamwork.

- Celebrate "please" and "thank you." Select a day and declare it "Please and Thank You Day." Have a bowl of pennies and a jar available. When someone fails to say the appropriate phrase, require them to put a penny in the jar, changing a larger coin if necessary. Based on the size of the department or organization, decide what is an acceptable number of pennies to declare the day a success. If less than that number is found in the jar, celebrate. If more, try the exercise again the next month and see if you can improve the response. At the next staff-volunteer meeting explore how everyone felt during and after the exercise.

- If you have not already done so, put your volunteers on the list to receive any information sent to employees about what is going on in the organization — upcoming events, new programs, personnel changes, etc. Your volunteers wanted to become a part of something. Make them feel they truly are. One idea would be to create a separate, private Facebook group for your volunteer program. Besides giving your volunteers a venue for communication with the organization and each other, the group site can share information about upcoming events, highlight specific volunteers for recognition among their peers, or simply to share words of encouragement.

- Hold occasional brainstorming sessions with staff and volunteers on ways to improve office procedures or client services. Try to direct conversation so ideas are built upon: something an employee suggests triggers an idea to make the employee's idea better or something the volunteer says triggers a suggestion that enhances the idea from a staff member. The goal is to establish a culture of teamwork.

- If the pace of work does not give volunteers a chance to understand what is going on beyond their limited assignment, provide periodic informal gatherings, perhaps with refreshments, so the staff can bring volunteers up to date on what is going on in their department, or how what they are doing fits into the bigger picture of the organization's work. This will also allow volunteers to raise questions that staff has been too busy to address, or the volunteers have been too busy to ask. Incomplete information or not understanding what is going on prevents the volunteer from feeling an important part of the operation. These things could also cause volunteers to make unnecessary mistakes.

- Invite volunteers to put their suggestions in the suggestion box. Make sure they get a response that either acknowledges their suggestion, or shows appreciation but explains why the suggestion cannot be instituted. If it is the policy of the organization to acknowledge the best suggestions, make sure volunteers are represented in the winners.

- Prepare a small printed guide for employees suggesting ways they can help make volunteers more comfortable in your organization. The guide should stress the importance of engaging volunteers in conversation, including them in activities, remembering to say thank you, and other ideas on how the employee can help integrate the volunteer into the culture of the organization.

- Have a brown bag day once a month. Invite all the volunteers to join the staff for lunch and conversation.

- If you have short-term volunteers, end their period of volunteering with a staff-hosted thank you event — lunch, a small party, whatever suits the structure of your organization. Thank the volunteer for the help and be sure to invite them back to volunteer again when they have the time.

- Hold an in-house pool. When you have a project that is being done under pressure with the help of volunteers, hold a pool where everyone guesses the date and time the project will be completed, and arrange for a humorous prize for the person that comes closest.

- Find out if any of your volunteers share any interests or hobbies with people on your staff. If you find any connections put the people together.

- Institute a policy that employees spend at least 10 minutes at the beginning of a volunteer's shift to catch up on the latest news about the volunteer's family, hobbies, or other interests. Encourage the employee to share something that happened in their life since they last saw the volunteer.

- Set a policy that any staff member who works with a volunteer makes a point of saying goodbye to them at the end of their shift, and thanks them for his or her help.

CHAPTER **10**:

SETTING YOUR VOLUNTEERS UP TO SUCCEED

Why would a nonprofit looking for long-term commitment set their volunteers up for failure? As illogical as this may sound, it does happen — not intentionally, of course. It happens when a nonprofit fails to adequately support its volunteers.

A volunteer brings his or her energy and heart to a nonprofit with the expectation the organization will provide the training, information, and support — both practical and emotional — the volunteer needs to put these gifts to productive use. Unfortunately, according to a recent study of nonprofit management policies, this does not always happen.

The study found while nearly half of the nonprofits in the sample had some management policy about providing training and professional development opportunities for their volunteers, only 25 percent adopted the practice to "any large degree." Failure to provide volunteers with an opportunity to develop and grow with your organization sends the message you see them as temporary or occasional help, not as a critical part of your organization's future. This is not a message you want to send if you are looking for long-term commitment. Your volunteers are there because they want to work and grow. They want and expect to be challenged.

"There is only one thing worse than training a volunteer and having them leave. That is not training a volunteer and having them stay."

— Anonymous

Volunteers Want and Need to Be Challenged

"If work is not meaningful, do not ask volunteers to do it. Volunteers need to know that their contribution is important. They find time to work on projects that contribute to goals that they support. They are motivated when they gain in some way — a new skill, new relationships, a feeling that what they did made a difference. Volunteers are more likely to complete tasks and do so on time when they know that others are counting on them."

— Helen Little, *Volunteers: How To Get Them, How To Keep Them*

David Geary spent 16 years as the director of Universal Studio's highly successful volunteer disaster response team, a part of the studio's emergency services program. While Universal Studios is a for-profit organization, the volunteer disaster response team Geary created and directed operates along the same lines as any nonprofit volunteer program. Except for the director and a professional trainer, all the participants are volunteers who take on their team responsibilities in addition to their paid work assignments.

The program was created in response to a serious concern. Universal Studio sits on a 400-acre campus in Universal City near Burbank, California. The studio's 250 buildings house more than 8,000 employees. Add to this the tens of thousands of tourists who visit the studio's entertainment park on any given day, and the possibility of chaos in the event of an earthquake, fire, or terrorist attack is evident.

During his tenure, Geary trained and supervised a group of 400 Universal employees to serve as disaster response team members and emergency wardens. In return for donating their time, the volunteers receive training that provided them with the skills and knowledge necessary to enable them to help their fellow employees and studio visitors in the event of a natural disaster or man-made emergency.

VOLUNTEER STORIES
FROM THE FIELD

David Geary, Former Director
Universal Studio's Disaster Response Program
Universal City, California
Current Contact Number: 847-526-9680

Universal Studio's Disaster Response Program trains employee-volunteers to assist fellow employees and visitors in the event of an emergency. During a typical year these volunteers are required to complete 15-25 hours of specialized training.

Report from: David Geary, program developer and former director

There is no room for operating at a poor quality level in any organization, and it should not be acceptable in a volunteer organization either. Any organization will fail if it cannot accomplish its mission routinely. Even if it should manage to survive, the organization's poor reputation will make it difficult to recruit and retain the high-quality volunteers necessary to sustain it, because people who volunteer do so out of a desire to become a part of something good.

When I set out to develop the volunteer disaster response team program for Universal Studios, I decided the best way to achieve high-quality results was through mandatory levels of training and participation. To avoid poor performance, I set high standards. Volunteers who had difficulty meeting those standards were counseled for success. In time, the program became self-sustaining and is still running with the volunteers helping out with leadership, training, and recruitment duties.

The challenge that confronts volunteer managers is to have sufficient courage to make requirements and mandatory participation levels a part of their organization's core values so they can uphold the quality of the organization. Having a reputation for quality is essential for attracting and keeping the high-quality volunteers necessary to sustain an organization.

Providing quality training and setting high standards that challenge volunteers and create an opportunity for personal growth are two ways for an organization to support its volunteers. The most frequent excuse nonprofits give for not doing these things is a lack of money or a lack of time. However, failing to provide your volunteers with adequate support, whatever the reason, will set them up for failure.

When the Volunteer Assignment Offers No Challenge

According to countless studies on what volunteers seek, today's volunteers are searching for meaning and purpose. Professionals who consult on the subject will tell you the best way to help volunteers find the purpose they are seeking in your organization is to place them in assignments that match their skills, talents, and interests and provide them with an opportunity for personal growth. However, this is not always possible. There are inevitably jobs that need to be done that require little skill and offer no challenge.

It is easy to point out the value of a volunteer assignment that has a discernible impact, as in training people to step forward in an emergency. There is an obvious payoff for these volunteers: They experience pride and satisfaction in the performance of their work. The challenge is with the essential menial chores frequently assigned to volunteers — they needed to be presented in such a way that volunteers can see their meaning or purpose.

Four Elements of an Appropriate "Thank You" for Mundane Tasks

1. Sincere recognition of the tedious nature of the task.

2. Reinforcement that the assignment does not reflect the organization's view of the volunteer's value or capabilities.

3. Specific illustration of how or why the task is important to organization's mission.

4. Expression of gratitude that the volunteer was willing to undertake the mundane task for the sake of the organization.

To accomplish this, the volunteer manager needs to take the time to point out the connection between the volunteer's assignment and the organization's mission. And they need to reinforce this connection every time they thank the volunteer for his or her help — which should be every time the volunteer comes in to work and at the completion of the volunteer's work period.

An appropriate "thank you" for a mundane assignment has four elements. It should acknowledge the volunteer manager's understanding that the task the volunteer has been assigned is boring and unchallenging.

The second thing your "thank you" should do is address the feelings being saddled with such an unchallenging and boring assignment can trigger. Except for the most confident among us, it is human nature for individuals to draw their sense of personal value from the work they do, and to believe others judge their value on the same basis. It is important that you make it clear to your volunteer that you recognize the job does not make the best use of all his or her skills and talents. You can turn this deficit — the unchallenging nature of the job — into a benefit by praising the volunteer's generosity in accepting this unchallenging assignment for the good of the organization and its mission.

The third element your "thank you" should contain is a reminder the volunteer's job makes an important contribution to the organization's ability to accomplish its mission. If the job is inputting information into the computer, you might point out how this information is critical to obtaining funding or complying with government regulations. If the task has to do with folding, stamping or stuffing mailers, you could point out the amount of money such mailings usually bring in, or the number of people the agency is frequently able to help because of such mailings. If the volunteer is assisting with general clerical work, take the time to explain how their help has enabled the organization to free up a member of the staff to attend to important tasks that might have been neglected or abandoned without the volunteer's willingness to help. The more specific you can be, the more clearly your volunteer will understand how their seemly unimportant work relates to the success of the organization.

And finally, the "thank you" should express your personal gratitude, and the gratitude of the organization, that the volunteer has so graciously taken on this mundane assignment.

This is not to suggest the "thank you" should be a recitation of the four elements. These four points are guidelines to keep in mind when you solicit feedback from your volunteer about the routine assignment you have given him or her; they are suggestions to help you shape a conversation that will set a tone of appreciation and encouragement designed to make the volunteer more comfortable with the assignment.

Supporting Volunteer Success with Knowledge

Volunteers come to their tasks with the best of intentions, but occasionally their life experiences have not equipped them sufficiently to handle the tasks they have volunteered to take on. This sometimes happens when volunteers work with an agency's clients.

While you always have the option of aborting a project that does not appear to be working out, as a volunteer manager you want your volunteers to succeed; you want to be able to provide the support they need to succeed. This was the position Danielle Kearney of Lutheran Services Florida found herself in when she received a call from a member of one of her volunteer church groups.

 **VOLUNTEER STORIES FROM THE FIELD**

 Lutheran Services Florida
3627A W. Waters Ave.
Tampa, Florida
Website: **www.lsfnet.org**

Lutheran Services Florida (LSF) is a statewide, nonprofit, human service agency dedicated to helping people in need regardless of religious affiliation, age, or country of origin. The agency offers more than 60 programs located throughout Florida and uses thousands of volunteers in times of a disaster. They use volunteers for office work, community outreach, and client and program support.

Report from Danielle Kearney, director, Church and Community Relations

We had a church group of volunteers working with a refugee family. One of the volunteers from the group called the office complaining that the refugee family they were working with would not eat canned food, but wanted everything fresh. It was clear from the conversation that the volunteer group had become disenchanted with the family.

We took the time to go to the church and meet with the volunteers, and educate them on the eating habits and culture of the refugee family. We explained that the family did not have canned goods in their home country. However, we told the group that it would be good for the volunteers to teach the refugees to cook using canned goods.

The church group ended up making this a fun experience and in the process taught the refugees how to use coupons and get bargains. This was a simple situation, but in many cases using common sense and talking with the volunteers can help solve problems.

The Benefits of Cultural Diversity and Sensitivity Training

If your organization serves immigrant populations or populations whose cultural background differs from that of most of your volunteers, you should consider adding a course in cultural diversity to your ongoing volunteer training program. There are many advantages to doing this.

Most importantly, this type of training would help equip your volunteers with the understanding they need for successful interaction with your clients. The educational nature of the training would also satisfy the desire many volunteers have to realize personal growth from their volunteer experience. And opening the course to all volunteers — even those who do not work with clients — and to your staff, would enable you to put a human face on your mission, which will help these volunteers and employees connect emotionally with the work they do. Such an emotional connection frequently results in increased commitment.

If your agency works with physically or mentally challenged clients, the elderly, or children, you may want to include sensitivity training in your ongoing volunteer training program. The more tools you can provide for your volunteers, the better chance they will have to succeed.

> "We pride ourselves on first asking the question of our volunteers: 'What do you want to do?' And then we match up their passion, skills, and interests with our needs second. We have found that when a volunteer is doing what they want — if they find it to be personally satisfying — then it typically is a good experience for them, and a lot of fun, particularly when their chemistry with their staff partner is as positive!"
> — **Lauren Perlmutter**, Director, Volunteer Leadership Development, March of Dimes

How March of Dimes Promotes Volunteer Success

One organization that has put a great deal of thought into how to help their volunteers succeed is the March of Dimes.

Having their volunteers succeed is, in fact, the main focus of their approach with volunteers, and has spawned a philosophy that views volunteers not as some vast collection of potential help, but as individuals with specific talents to be recognized, respected, and used effectively to advance the organization's mission to improve the health of babies.

The organization's perspective of volunteers is remarkable given the **scope of March of Dimes' donor base: 3,000 chapter and division board members and more than 3 million volunteers.**

March of Dimes' volunteer program did not just happen; it is the result of research and strategic planning. Needs were analyzed; ways to find and mobilize the talent needed to meet those needs were explored; and dollar value of volunteers was calculated. The result is a program that effectively uses volunteers for all aspects of the organization's mission including research, education, advocacy, community services, and most importantly fund raising.

To attract and keep these valuable volunteers engaged, March of Dimes translated its philosophy into a collection of challenging training programs that educate their volunteers about the organization and help them develop and strengthen their leadership skills. One of the things that sets March of Dimes apart from many other nonprofits is the concept that volunteers

— all volunteers — are potential leaders. Here is a quick look at some of the things they do to help their volunteers fulfill this potential:

- They begin with a well-crafted orientation program that combines a uniform presentation that clearly defines March of Dimes' history and mission; a local presentation that familiarizes the new volunteers with the special characteristics and challenges of the geographic area in which they will be working; and introduces them to the regional and local March of Dimes leadership.

- They reinforce their orientation with periodic training sessions that cover specific March of Dimes leadership issues, such as the role and responsibilities of volunteer leaders.

- They recruit volunteers with specialized skills in areas such as strategic planning, marketing, information technology, and training and research to support and supplement the work of their limited paid staff. This practice enables March of Dimes to access valuable expertise it could not otherwise afford. It also provides the organization with an opportunity to create the kind of challenging and rewarding volunteer opportunities that attract quality volunteers and promotes loyalty and long-term commitment.

- They promote leadership development for volunteers through their March of Dimes Volunteer Leadership Conference. The institute includes internally and externally developed training courses, best practices, and tools and resources for March of Dimes volunteer leaders. It is guided by the National Volunteer Leadership Institute Council.

- March of Dimes' Volunteer Leadership Institute provides retreats, webinar programs, and web-based tools for volunteers that can be found online at **www.marchofdimes. com/volunteerland.**

Most nonprofits will never deal with thousands of volunteers or need to set up a leadership institute, but the philosophy that guides March of Dimes in its use and treatment of volunteers provides a useful template that nonprofits of any size or focus can use to help their volunteers enjoy and succeed in their volunteer experience.

How to Create a Program That Fosters Volunteer Success

What does success look like to a volunteer? It expresses itself in a sense of competence. Whether the task involves inputting information, delivering magazines to hospital patients, or fundraising, if the volunteer feels he or she has been well prepared and is performing the task competently, the volunteer will feel successful.

Volunteers feel successful when the organization or the clients they work with acknowledge their services and make them feel valued and appreciated. Volunteers also feel successful when they face a challenge and know they have met it.

Success is addictive. You want your volunteers to experience it because they will want to repeat the experience, which will result in an extended commitment. Therefore, you want to create a volunteer program that provides as much opportunity as possible for your volunteers to succeed.

- **Begin by assessing and, if necessary, modifying your organization's perception of the place and purpose of volunteers in relation to its work and mission.** One characteristic that sets organizations with successful volunteer programs apart is their astute understanding of the possibilities inherent in a volunteer. Too many nonprofits are ensnared by the historic meaning of the word — a free source of help — which in no way begins to suggest the vast resource of skills and experiences today's volunteers can bring to an organization. March of Dimes understands this. So does the American Cancer Society, which refers to its volunteers as "talent" and the head of its volunteer program as chief talent officer. The department that deals with the recruitment and coordination of volunteer activity is known as "Talent Strategy." Would referring to your volunteers by another term give your staff a different perspective of them, or open up new possibilities for the more effective deployment of volunteers? What would happen if you referred to them as "mission partners" or "staff support" instead of volunteers?

- **Engage in strategic planning.** It is common practice among nonprofits to create volunteer positions in response to current needs. In the for-profit world this practice would be classified as crisis management. A rich resource like volunteers deserves a more thoughtful approach. Instead of letting urgent needs shape your volunteer program, build your program with strategic planning. Before you recruit, analyze your operation to determine where or how you might be able to improve or expanded your services by adding professional skills. Budget limitations may prevent you from hiring someone to provide these skills, but you can acquire them by designing creative part-time volunteer positions that will attract individuals with the talents you need. If you are unsuccessful recruiting the right person through traditional channels or personal contacts, try the internet. Websites such as **www.idealist.org, www. volunteermatch.com,** and **http://volunteer.truist.com** can help you connect with retired management executives, computer technicians, accountants, and advertising and public relations professionals looking to volunteer for a worthy cause. A strategically planned volunteer program enables you to create a richer selection of volunteer positions to provide your volunteers with more opportunities for challenge and personal growth.

- **Move volunteer training to the top of your list of necessities.** Volunteer training should be an ongoing process that goes beyond preparing a volunteer for their initial assignment. Training sessions could be designed to encourage leadership within a volunteer team, to give volunteers a deeper understanding of the organization's mission, or to train volunteers to move into different levels of the volunteer program. Using training programs in these ways will challenge and engage your volunteers and keep their volunteering experience fresh and rewarding.

- **Expect and encourage excellence.** In business or socially, people are insulted when we approach them with low expectations. Volunteers are no different. To accept inferior work because the person who did the work was "just a volunteer" is to imply volunteers are not capable of good work. Set high standards, provide help if your volunteer has trouble meeting those standards, but do not deprive them of the challenge or the possibility of achieving a level of excellence. And do not forget to acknowledge their accomplishment when they succeed.

- **Give your volunteers some place to grow in your organization.** Some people are more comfortable doing the same thing over and over again, but most people tend to lose interest once they master a skill or situation. Design your volunteer opportunities so you can offer a progression of work that will give your volunteers the opportunity to grow within your organization.

- **Structure your volunteer jobs so a volunteer can alternate tedious assignments with more interesting and challenging assignments.** This is sometimes difficult to do, but does help keep volunteers engaged while enabling you to get routine work accomplished.

One final thought: Even in the best planned program, some volunteers taking on an assignment that places them in unfamiliar territory are bound to fail. If it is just a matter of helping the volunteer learn how to do the assignment, be a cheerleader during the learning process. If it becomes obvious the job is beyond the volunteer's skill level, find them another assignment more suited to their abilities and support their success in the new job. Promoting a culture of excellence and success within your volunteer program will create the kind of volunteer experience that fosters long-term commitment.

Tips for Building a Success-Oriented Volunteer Culture

- Expect excellence. Holding your volunteers to high standards is a sign of respect. To excuse inferior performance because they are "just volunteers" sets your volunteers up for failure.

- Success is addictive. If you can give your volunteers a successful experience they will want to repeat it, which will eventually lead to long-term commitments and a stable volunteer program.

- By setting high standards for volunteers your organization gains a reputation for being a quality operation. This, in turn, attracts high-quality volunteers who help your organization sustain its good reputation.

- Creating volunteer positions only to fill immediate needs is crisis management, which is unproductive in the for-profit world and equally wasteful in the nonprofit arena.

- Nonprofits use strategic planning to fulfill their mission and plan their growth, but seldom include volunteer recruitment and management in their plan. However, volunteers are one of a nonprofit's most valuable and versatile resources. Volunteer recruitment and management should be an integral part of any nonprofit's strategic planning.

- The quickest way to discourage volunteers is to provide them with bland, unchallenging volunteer opportunities.

- There is no great mystery to figuring out what keeps volunteers engaged. Put yourself in their place and decide what would keep you coming back.

- Being concerned that you will lose volunteers if your requirements and training are too demanding is counter-intuitive. You are more likely to lose volunteers if you fail to challenge them. Those volunteers who have difficulty meeting the required high standards should be counseled to help them succeed.

- Volunteer assignments should be periodically evaluated from the volunteer's prospective as well as the staff's perspective. In addition to meeting with the volunteers individually, meet with them as a group, and focus the feedback session on ways to improve the volunteer experience for your volunteers. Meeting as a group opens the possibility of a cross-pollination of ideas.

- Consider setting up a volunteer assignment swap program. Give volunteers the opportunity to swap assignments after a period of time to expand their experience with the organization.

- Establish an ongoing training program that enables volunteers to deepen their experience with your organization by expanding the possible ways they can become involved. Some examples of programs are a training program that gives volunteers the opportunity to improve their speaking and presentation skills and provides them with a deeper understanding of your organization; a training program that opens the door for volunteers wishing to become fundraisers; or a program that trains volunteers to move from staff support to working with clients.

- Have occasional informal volunteer gatherings to allow volunteers to discuss their successes within the volunteer program. The success might be an innovation a volunteer introduced that improved the efficiency of the office operation; a volunteer's completion of a challenging training program; or a breakthrough a volunteer made with a client. The objective is to support volunteer success wherever it occurs.

- Use social media to your advantage. Sharing items such as photos of volunteers or information about upcoming events can create interest in the community outside of those already involved with the organization. Creating a private group Facebook page can be a wonderful means of building a bond between the volunteers as well as a site for sharing information and success stories in-house.

- Organizations that deal with the homeless, the physically or mentally challenged, or with poor, immigrant communities should consider adding a relevant cultural education program to their range of training program for volunteers. The program should be made available to all volunteers, not just those who work directly with clients. Such programs provide a deeper understanding of the client and the mission. They also foster a sense of involvement for the volunteers and an opportunity for personal growth.

- Make arrangements for one of the organization's financial officers to make a presentation to staff-support volunteers. You might want to include paid staff. Have the financial officer discuss the relationship between the ability of the organization to meet its financial and legal obligation and the work done by the office staff and volunteers. The presentation should conclude with a "thank you" to the volunteers for helping to keep the office running smoothly so the organization can focus on its mission.

- Ask your volunteers how they would like to be recognized: Would they prefer being considered mission partners, mission supporters, or staff support? Use this meeting to acknowledge that you recognize they are far more than free help. Let them know the organization appreciates the valuable skills and talents they bring to the mission.

- Consider following the practice of Universal Giving: once you have volunteers onboard and they have become familiar with your organization, tell them what your needs are and give them the opportunity to design their own volunteer assignment. This should be done with guidance from someone on staff who has the understanding and the skill to help shape the proposed assignment so it meets both the organization's and the volunteer's needs.

- Introduce a volunteer suggestion box and request suggestions for new volunteer opportunities that might improve the efficiency, service, or effectiveness of the organization.

- Develop a four-point "thank you" for volunteers saddled with unchallenging jobs: (1) Acknowledge the mundane nature of the work; (2) Reinforce the fact the organization understands the job does not reflect the volunteer's capabilities; (3) Connect the job to the organization's ability to fulfill its mission; and (4) Thank the volunteer for their generosity in accepting such a mundane assignment for the good of the organization.

- Devote a corner of the office or volunteer bulletin board — plus exposure via your social media presence — to "Volunteer Success Stories," and every week or month (depending on the size of your organization) post a story and picture about a volunteer's success in handling a situation. The story might be about beating a deadline, getting an impressive donation, or coming up with a money-saving way to do something.

- Tune into your volunteers' passions and create opportunities that give your volunteers the chance to employ those passions in their volunteer work. For example: ask a volunteer who enjoys doing calligraphy to address invitations for special fundraising events. Church volunteers who like to knit or crochet can be invited to make prayer shawls for congregants with health problems or who are undergoing personal tragedies. An agency that works with underprivileged children or homeless families might invite volunteers who enjoy knitting to make mufflers and mittens to be given to clients around the winter holidays. A community outreach organization might enlist volunteers who enjoy doing handy work to do minor repairs for elderly citizens in the community. Being able to combine the pursuit of a passion with the practice of helping others makes for a memorable and rewarding volunteer experience.

- Research done by The Corporation for National and Community Service (CNCS) found volunteers who engage in less challenging activities tend to be less likely to continue volunteering the following year. This is a good argument for creating challenging volunteer opportunities.

- If you want your volunteers to feel their services make a difference, you are going to have to demonstrate the impact those services have on your organization's mission in concrete terms your volunteer can understand.

- Be willing to break the mold. If you cannot afford to hire a well-qualified individual to run your volunteer department, do what the American Red Cross did — find a highly qualified volunteer to oversee the department's volunteers and paid staff.

- Volunteers tend to be more comfortable working in an

environment where they are given equal value with paid staff. If there is a distinct separation between volunteers and staff in your organization, consider equalizing the situation by having volunteers and staff go through orientation and training together. Foster the feeling volunteers are partners with staff, and in pursuit of the same goals.

• Create a culture of success in your volunteer program by providing the training and emotional support your volunteers need to succeed.

CHAPTER 11:

EMPOWERING VOLUNTEERS

To succeed, volunteers need to be supported; to want to stay, they also need to be empowered. Anyone who has ever worked with volunteers knows this is true. Why then are some nonprofits reluctant to incorporate this truth into their management practices? Frequently the reason has to do with control.

Operating a nonprofit means learning to live with uncertainty. Income sources that appeared secure when the budget was prepared can dry up overnight through no fault of the organization. Suddenly goals need to be adjusted, plans need to be changed, and the staff needs to be juggled. Therefore, in the one area the nonprofit can maintain control — their volunteer program — its boards and managers are sometimes reluctant to commit wholeheartedly to the empowerment of its volunteers. Unfortunately, reluctance to make this commitment can be a major stumbling block for an organization trying to convince its volunteers to make long-term commitments. As with most aspects of volunteer management, a nonprofit must find a way to strike a balance between its understandable desire to maintain control and its need to empower its volunteers.

"An empowered organization is one in which individuals have the knowledge, skill, desire, and opportunity to personally succeed in a way that leads to collective organizational success."

— **Stephen R. Covey,** author of *The 7 Habits of Highly Effective People*

Defining Volunteer Empowerment

Striking that balance becomes easier when you understand empowering volunteers does not mean giving them control; it means making them partners in the pursuit of your mission. To do this frequently means helping your volunteers recognize their own strengths and potential and encouraging them to employ these on behalf of your mission. This ability is at the center of a successful Habitat for Humanity program in Washington State underwritten by Thrivent Financial for Lutherans. Here is a report from the program's volunteer coordinator, Barbara Price.

VOLUNTEER STORIES FROM THE FIELD

Thrivent Builds with Habitat for Humanity
Cowlitz County Habitat for Humanity (CCHFH)
Longview, Washington
Website: **www.cowlitzhabitat.org**

Cowlitz County Habitat for Humanity, a part of Thrivent Financial for Lutherans/ Thrivent Builds with Habitat for Humanity program, provides "decent, affordable housing for low income families and individuals." CCHFH's volunteers are involved in fund raising, construction teams, support for construction teams (devotions, lunches, and snacks), volunteer recruitment, publicity, and administrative support.

Report from Barbara Price, volunteer coordinator

I have found it helpful to encourage them to give leadership roles a try, and to support their efforts by accompanying them to meetings and speaking engagements (public speaking or asking for donations). I believe in respecting an individual's option to say no. I encourage individuals to say "no" if that is the best response for them. I encourage everyone to volunteer by praying for the success of the project. I do not ask volunteers to do anything I am not willing to do. As a result, volunteers come forth when they determine they can succeed, knowing someone will support and appreciate their efforts.

Seeing volunteers at the construction site partnering and supporting the partner family and the other volunteers, from teaching construction techniques to friendly competition between volunteer groups, my conclusion — which I constantly share — is you gain so much by participating in these projects that the organization should charge for the experience. The projects are fun for the volunteers because we incorporate recognition from the beginning with competitions within and between groups, T-shirts, pins, candy, and for the Lutherans, lots of good strong coffee.

Barbara Price points out another important key to empowering volunteers — listening. Her ability to hear when her volunteers say "no" and to respect that "no" builds trust because it lets her volunteers know they are being heard.

Listening: The Beginning of Empowerment

We have all had the experience, perhaps with a parent, a teacher, or a boss: Something happens and you want to explain or suggest a solution, but the other person refuses to take the time to listen, or is so invested in their own solution they dismiss anything you have to say. Do you remember how frustrated and powerless that made you feel?

When a volunteer's suggestions and ideas are ignored or rebuffed they begin to shut down. The emotional bond that individual had begun to build with the organization starts to unravel. The volunteer may complete his or her commitment, but it will not be with the same enthusiasm. Once their commitment has been met, if not sooner, the volunteer will probably leave. All this can be avoided by making "active listening" a policy of your volunteer program.

An active listener does not simply listen; he or she becomes engaged in the experience. There are five steps involved in active listening:

1. **Establish eye contact.** Whether the volunteer approaches you or you approach the volunteer, the first thing you want to do is establish eye contact with him or her to let him or her know they have your attention.

2. **Stay focused.** Ignore distractions and stay focused on what is being said, nodding occasionally to let the volunteer know you are listening.

3. **Ask insightful questions.** Ask pertinent questions to reassure the volunteer you are hearing him or her. Clarify or verify what you have heard to make sure you have understood what has been said.

4. **Take appropriate action.** If all that is required is a simple answer, provide it. If further action is required, confirm that you will take it.

5. **Say thank you.** Depending on the situation, thank the volunteer for the information, their concern, or their suggestion — whatever is appropriate.

A word of warning: No matter how well you master and practice the art of active listening, if step four only results in empty promises — if you fail to follow through — your volunteer will feel betrayed instead of empowered. Never make a commitment to a volunteer you cannot or do not intend to keep.

Inclusion: A Powerful Tool for Empowering Volunteers

Volunteers are empowered when they are made to feel they are an important part of your organization and when they believe their voice is being heard. Accomplishing this is not something the volunteer coordinator can do alone. It requires the cooperation of staff, management, and the other volunteers. Because the tone of a volunteer's tenure is established during orientation, your policy of inclusion and your organization's practice of welcoming volunteer input needs to be clearly stated in your welcoming statement. It should also be reinforced by your management and board personally as they greet and welcome each new volunteer.

Once a new volunteer has been on the job long enough to become familiar with your program, they should have an informal meeting with the volunteer manager. This meeting should be in addition to the volunteer's evaluation meeting.

During this informal session invite the volunteer to share his or her observations about the program: What do they think is working well? What suggestions do they have for improving those areas of the program they feel are not working well? The volunteer's suggestions should always be given consideration. If these suggestions are useful and can be implemented, they should be incorporated into your program. If it would not be feasible to act on the suggestions, take the time to explain why. The important thing is to let the volunteer know he or she has been heard and their feedback is helpful and appreciated.

Here are some others ideas for ways to empower your volunteers through inclusion:

- Include your volunteers in staff mailings, emails, and private Facebook group posts relating to the inner workings of the organization. This might include weekly updates on projects, notices about upcoming events, summaries of board meetings provided to staff, or copies of the organization's annual report.

- Spotlight your volunteers' organization-related successes and any personal recognition they get from other civic or church affiliations in your internal employee/donor publications.

- Have a "Help Make Us Better" event periodically for volunteers or volunteers and staff to brainstorm ways to make the volunteer program (or organization) more effective and productive.

- Inform your volunteers about upcoming events before they are announced to the general public.

- Ask for volunteer input on events that are being planned.

- Invite volunteers to take part in the debriefing after an event so they can provide feedback and suggestions on how to improve future events.

- Respond to suggestions volunteers put in the suggestion box with a thank you note. If possible, include a comment on why your organization will or will not be able to implement the suggestion.

- Have an experienced staff member help guide your new volunteer through the first couple weeks of their volunteer experience. By providing insight into the organization and how the volunteer program works, the staff member can help the volunteer move from uncertain newcomer to confident insider more quickly.

- Get in the habit of acknowledging volunteers at outreach events with specific reference to something they have done for the organization.

- Have your board president or executive director establish a practice of sending a personal, handwritten thank you note or congratulatory note to volunteers who accomplished anything that warrants recognition from the organization. The contents of the note should reinforce the idea this volunteer is a valuable asset to the organization.

- Provide an attractive, comfortable spot in your offices for your volunteers to relax, check in, or attend to their paperwork.

- Use a cheat-sheet if necessary, but remember your volunteer's name, the names of his or her children, spouse or significant other, and a connecting detail about his or her life so you always have a conversation starter available.

- Create a volunteer honor roll and publish it on your website.

The last suggestion was inspired by Ami Simms, founder of the Alzheimer's Quilt Initiative, a grassroots volunteer-run nonprofit based in Burton, Michigan, that effectively uses the internet as an empowerment tool for its more than 1,500 volunteers across the United States. Here is what Simms has to say about empowering volunteers:

VOLUNTEER STORIES FROM THE FIELD

 1200 Creek wood Trail
Burton, Michigan
Website: www.AlzQuilts.org

The Alzheimer's Art Quilt Initiative is an internet-driven, grassroots, all-volunteer effort to raise awareness of Alzheimer's disease and fund research through art, specifically through quilting.

Report from Ami Simms, founder and executive director, Art Quilt Initiative

Transparency is one way we empower our volunteers. We try to show them every facet of our organization so they feel part of it. This increases trust and ensures good stewardship of funds earned from their efforts. Welcoming suggestions is another way. Not only do we welcome their suggestions, but we try to incorporate them in our programs and policies.

For example, one of our volunteers suggested we create a place where quilt donors could pledge to donate as many quilts as it took individually to raise $1,000. Her ingenuity was responsible for a program that has helped to raise thousands of dollars. Almost 70 people have joined it. Some have fulfilled their pledge many times over. We acknowledge our appreciation by honoring these volunteers on our website.

Keeping your mind open to what your volunteers propose is crucial. They have great ideas! Empowering them to use their creativity to drive the organization is critical.

The following was posted on the Alzheimer's Art Quilt website, followed by an honor roll list of volunteers who participated in the $1,000 Promise Project and the amount each volunteer raised.

The Alzheimer's Art Quilt Initiative (AAQI)
Raising Awareness & Funding Research
Through Art www.AlzQuilts.org

$1,000 Promise

The following people have pledged to raise $1,000 through the sale or auction of Priority: Alzheimer's Quilts they donate. They feel so strongly about their promise, they have asked that their names be listed here to inspire others to take up the challenge. Very special thanks to Joanne Guillemette for suggesting this grand idea and high fives to everyone who is willing to join her!

To pledge your support, email Diane with your name, city, state, and a short statement about why you are making this very generous pledge. A web page will be created for you below. Please note that only Priority: Alzheimer's Quilts count toward the $1,000 Promise.

We ask that you please help Diane keep track of your quilts. Please email Diane when the photo appears by your quilt on the Waiting For Assignment page and again when it is sold. Always refer to your quilts by their numbers. The more often you check your page, the faster it will be updated.

The dollar amount below each name indicates the amount the quilt has earned. The fraction appearing by the individual's name indicates the number of quilts sold (top number) and the number of quilts donated (bottom number). Only registered quilts which have had their photographs taken and processed will appear here. (There is a short lag time between registration and appearance on the web page.)

Incredibly generous individuals and businesses have stepped forward to encourage quilters making and donating Priority: Alzheimer's Quilts to raise money for Alzheimer's research by awarding very special prizes when they fulfill their $1,000 Promise.

Team Building as a Tool for Empowerment

The word "team" suggests synergy, which is defined as a common vision or shared purpose that overrides personal interests. These are precisely the characteristics one would expect to find in a team of volunteers and paid staff working together to support a nonprofit's mission. In fact, many for-profit corporations promote volunteering to their employees because they believe giving them an opportunity to work together outside their normal work environment on a volunteer project builds team spirit. Yet one of the reasons former volunteers frequently give for their decision to stop volunteering suggests not all nonprofits provide a satisfying team experience. These volunteers point to a lack of peer support and camaraderie as a contributing factor in their decision not to continue volunteering.

Disenchantment can set in quickly when a new volunteer is met with indifference or falls prey to pettiness or hurtful gossip. Even though such behavior seems incompatible with the concept of volunteering, it does occur. The best way to avoid these problems is to build your volunteers and the staff they work with into a cohesive team characterized by mutual respect and a sincere desire to provide support for each other. There is no better way to empower your volunteers than by providing this kind of nurturing work environment.

"Teamwork represents a set of values that encourages behaviors such as listening, constructively responding to points of view expressed by others, giving others the benefit of the doubt, providing support for those who need it, and recognizing the interests and achievements of others."

— J. R. Katznbach & D.K. Smith, *The Wisdom of Teams: Creating High Performance Organizations*

Team Building in a Volunteer Program

There is a marked difference between team building in the for-profit world and team building in a volunteer program. Corporations and other for-profit entities create teams to complete projects or increase staff productivity. The team members usually share a company culture and work together toward a common goal. The payoff is the successful accomplishment of that goal.

Team building in a volunteer program is more complex. Volunteer team members may work on different projects with different time frames and goals. They frequently come from diverse backgrounds and have varied levels of training and experience. A nonprofit team may consist of volunteers or a combination of volunteers and salaried staff, and the time commitment of the members may vary greatly. But the main difference between for-profit and nonprofit team building is their purpose. Unlike for-profit team building, the nonprofit is concerned more with the quality of the volunteer experience than what the team accomplishes. The primary purpose of team building in a volunteer program is to provide its volunteers with a more satisfying and empowering volunteer experience. Team building accomplishes this by strengthening the volunteer's sense of community within the organization.

There are three things needed to create a successful volunteer team:

- An agreed-upon rationale for working together

- A mutual commitment from all members of the team to be respectful and supportive of each other

- Strong leadership

A Rationale for Building a Volunteer Team

While group volunteering occurs through churches and civic organizations, the volunteers most nonprofits deal with are individuals who contribute their time with the hope they will find support and friendship once they begin working for the organization. Volunteer or combined volunteer-staff teams can help a nonprofit meet this expectation.

Team building can be applied to create a team from volunteers and staff members of a specific department, or to band together volunteers who share a common volunteer shift. It can be used to strengthen the relationships of volunteers on various campuses of a large nonprofit, or unify the volunteers of a small grassroots organization. Ideally a team should contain a combination of new and experienced volunteers so the more experienced volunteers provide help and encouragement to the newer volunteers.

The rationale for these volunteers to join together as a team is their shared desire to help the organization prosper and fulfill its mission. This is why they are all there — volunteer or staff. Working as a team, supporting each other, providing help and advice, sharing their trials and their triumphs — all this empowers the members of the team and helps them fulfill their volunteer commitment more efficiently. Just as important, the peer support and camaraderie the team generates makes the experience more satisfying and rewarding for everyone.

A Team Relationship Built on Mutual Commitment

Like any community, an effective team needs the structure bylaws provide to guide the interaction of its members. These bylaws should be developed by consensus and mutually agreed upon. The team's bylaws should state the goals and responsibilities of team members, define acceptable and unacceptable behavior, and establish a policy for handling conflicts. These team bylaws should reflect the organization's standards and philosophy focused through a narrower lens to address the specific relationship of team members.

> "In teamwork, silence isn't golden, it's deadly."
> — Mark Sanborn, *Teambuilt: Making Teamwork Work*

The Issue of Leadership

Every team needs a leader to provide direction, assure the implementation of the agreed-upon rules, and to keep team members on track. Depending on the situation, that leader could be the volunteer coordinator, or someone chosen from or elected by the team. If the team being formed includes a combination of clearly defined groups, two or three people representing the interests of those groups may assume leadership responsibilities.

Regardless of who takes on this responsibility, as a team leader he or she will want to try to create a safe, civil environment in which communication flows freely and honestly, and praise and concerns can be voiced with equal comfort. It will be up to the team leader to help the team maintain its vision and focus so all team members experience the sense of community and the support and encouragement they need to accomplish their tasks and enjoy their volunteer experience.

Volunteer Evaluation as an Empowerment Tool

Volunteers generously offer their gifts and time for free. This fact makes some volunteer managers uncomfortable with the idea of having to evaluate their volunteers' performance. Presenting the volunteer with a report card or critique of their work seems ungrateful. In reality, the opposite is true. Failure to evaluate a volunteer's work suggests low expectations and a lack of respect for the value of their time and effort — a far greater insult.

Your volunteers are there because they want to help. If they do a good job, they expect their accomplishment to be acknowledged. If they are doing work that is stretching their ability, they want feedback so they can learn how to meet the challenge and grow in the position. Both the acknowledgement of work well done and the supportive feedback from volunteer evaluations serve to empower your volunteers in their pursuit of a meaningful volunteer experience.

Whether you call it a volunteer evaluation, a performance assessment, or a work appraisal, a system that allows you to monitor and guide your volunteers' performance provides a powerful incentive for your volunteers to deepen their experience and make new commitments to your program.

Decision Sharing as an Empowerment Tool

There is a theory often voiced by people who work with volunteers that decisions should be made at the lowest possible level. The closer to the activity, the more effective the decision will be. Mike Wahl, deputy director of Emergency Management for the Wauconda Illinois Fire District, coordinates the area's all-volunteer Community Emergency Response Team (CERT). CERT is a nationwide program that trains and mobilizes local citizens to help in the event of a natural disaster or another emergency.

The program is divided into three tiers. Tier one is the initial training level — the 21-hour basic CERT class. Tier two is the team level in which the volunteers are issued equipment and uniforms and meet and train on a monthly basis. Tier three is the emergency management level that coordinates the activities of CERT volunteers. The members of this leadership team are handpicked from tier two.

The major challenge Wahl faces as volunteer coordinator for this program is keeping these volunteers, who range in age from 17 to 70 and come from diverse backgrounds, engaged, active, and motivated to keep up their training and participation in the program. His experience provides some insight into the value of giving volunteers some control over their volunteer experience.

VOLUNTEER STORIES FROM THE FIELD

CERT Program
Wauconda Fire District
Lake County, Illinois
Email: **MWahl@waucondafire.org**

The Wauconda Fire District's Community Emergency Response Team (CERT) program has one paid coordinator and 85 volunteers who undergo 21 hours of basic training and periodic on-going training to maintain their skills.

Report from Mike Wahl, volunteer coordinator for the Wauconda Fire District CERT Program

I think the most important thing we have done in our program is develop leadership and allow the membership to play an active role in deciding the direction of the program. The most important time was at the very conception of the program when we had our first 35 volunteers complete the class. After the class was completed we discussed the concept of the tier levels. From that point on we allowed the new volunteers to discuss how they felt the program should proceed. Many of the policies and procedures we use today are based on those initial discussions. I feel this has set the pace for our success.

Today, within our program, we have several work group committees. These committees plan their own meetings and work sessions. One example is our equipment committee that is responsible for all team equipment, as well as a fully equipped trailer. This working environment has provided strong fellowship.

Our CERT volunteers are an invaluable asset to our community. They enable us to supplement safety professional staffing needs for non-critical situations, freeing up our professional staff for more urgent duties. CERT brings the community together and allows people to become involved in things they would not normally have the opportunity to do.

While the structure of your volunteer program may not allow for providing your volunteers the same degree of autonomy, the concept of encouraging volunteers to participate in making decisions that affect their volunteer experience is applicable to any volunteer situation, and can be a powerful tool for empowering your volunteers.

But Wait! There is More: Your Best Empowerment Tool

We have just explored five tools to help you empower your volunteers: active listening, inclusion, team building, volunteer evaluation, and decision sharing. There is one more tool worth mentioning, perhaps the most important one of all: your attitude.

Nothing will inspire and empower your volunteers more than an attitude that demonstrates your faith in their ability to succeed. Nothing will grant you more loyalty from your volunteers than a positive, upbeat outlook that communicates your confidence they are doing a good job. It is not just what you do or say, but your body language, the smile on your face, and the joy they detect in your voice that inspires your volunteers to give their best. Good spirits are contagious. If your volunteers see you are enjoying working with them, they will enjoy working with you — the best motivation you can give them for committing to a long-term involvement with your organization.

Some Tips for Empowering Your Volunteers

Empowering volunteers is not about giving up power. It is about inviting your volunteers to partner with you in the pursuit of your mission by supporting and encouraging their efforts.

- Before you can empower someone, you need to learn to listen to them and truly hear what they are saying. This is the first step in empowerment.

- The technique of active listening requires five steps: (1) Maintaining eye contact to let   the other person know they have your attention; (2) Staying focused on what is being said and nodding occasionally to let him or her know you understand what he or she is saying; (3) Asking insightful questions and clarifying and confirming what the other party is saying; (4) Taking appropriate action; and (5) Thanking the other party for his or her information or suggestions.

- Never make a promise to your volunteers you cannot or do not intend to keep. Rather than being appeased, your volunteer will feel betrayed.

- If you pair a new volunteer with an experienced staff member for the first couple weeks of their service, the information your staff member shares based on their experience and knowledge of your organization can help speed up the volunteer's transition from uncomfortable newcomer to confident coworker.

- Transparency can be an empowerment tool. The more your volunteers understand about your organization and how it works, the more they will feel a part of it.

- Teamwork encourages beneficial behavior such as listening and constructively responding to the points of view others express; giving others the benefit of the doubt; providing support when needed; and recognizing the interests and achievements of others. All these qualities help to create a nurturing environment for a rewarding volunteer experience.

- Another way to empower your volunteers is to be sure they are comfortable with their assignments. Volunteers should receive clear, day-to-day instructions about their assigned tasks. They should know who to go to if they need additional instructions or clarification. Eliminating confusion is always empowering.

- Effective communication is key to empowering volunteers. Do not restrict your requests for feedback to formal meetings. Inquire about how your volunteers are doing informally whenever you see them.

- Giving your volunteers a comfortable, attractive spot in your offices to do their paperwork and relax speaks volumes about your perception of their value. The area does not have to be fancy, just uncluttered and reflecting care. This expression of your appreciation of them helps to empower them.

- Laughter should be encouraged in team gatherings. Laugher

lifts spirits, relieves tension, and promotes physical and mental good health. However, team leaders should stay alert to insensitive ethnic or racial humor that might offend some team members. A lapse of good judgment by a team member, even if unintentional, can seriously damage team harmony.

- In setting up your team, acknowledge the fact that teamwork can be difficult. Let your team members know what will be expected of them: Each team member needs to understand and commit to the goals and rules the team has agreed upon. Team members must be willing to acknowledge and confront conflict freely; respect individual differences; value the ideas and contributions of their fellow teammates; encourage them; and accept feedback from them graciously. Anything not worked for is seldom appreciated. Make it clear it will take work to make the team work. A team is not just a collection of people; it is a process of give and take.

- Consider occasionally including your volunteers in staff meetings that deal with subjects pertinent to their assignment. This will make them feel more a part of the department or organization.

- Volunteers can provide a fresh view of what went well or what went poorly in a public event. Include them in the debriefing after the event and invite them to share their insights and suggestions.

- Solicit volunteer input when planning a public event and encourage them to help with the preparation and execution of the event.

- Demonstrate that your organization sees your volunteers as whole people, valuable contributors, and not just extra hands to get work done. Celebrate their achievements in other arenas. Announce any recognition they receive from their religious or civic affiliations in your internal employee or donor publications. Have your board president or executive director send the volunteer a personal congratulatory note regarding the honor.

- Make volunteer evaluation a positive experience. If the volunteer has performed well, sincere praise is appropriate, but to be truly empowering, the volunteer should be encouraged to set new goals or consider new challenges. If the volunteer's performance has been less than hoped for, appreciation for their effort should be coupled with encouragement. The volunteer coordinator (or whomever conducts the evaluation) and the volunteer together should explore ideas for improving the volunteer's performance. If additional training or some form of mentoring would be helpful, this should be set up. The purpose of the evaluation is not to find fault, but to help the volunteer improve his or her performance, or envision new opportunities or challenges.

- Keep an open door. Your duties as volunteer coordinator can be relentless, but it is important your volunteers know they can come to you when they are troubled or unsure of something. Make a point of reminding them of this frequently. This will prevent mistakes and misunderstandings. An open-door policy is a small but empowering gesture that reminds your volunteers of their significance and your sincere wish to see them succeed.

- Almost everyone likes to be noticed. Rotate volunteer profiles on the volunteer page of your website. Every month feature a different volunteer, listing their recent accomplishments in your organization and in the outside world.

- Maintain a volunteer honor role. Nominations can come from staff, other volunteers, or clients. The honor roll can be posted in your office or on the internet. As a mark of their achievement, your board chair or executive director should follow up the announcement with a personal note of congratulations.

- Build team spirit by arranging social events for your teams. Depending on the make-up of the teams, they could be sports related, social gatherings, or group outings.

- In large organizations, good natured competition between teams could help build team morale and increase the fun of volunteering. The competition should be built around the interests of your teams: softball, volleyball, chess competitions, baking competitions, bridge tournaments — whatever will engage your volunteers. The more fun your volunteers are having as volunteers, the more empowered they will feel to expand their commitment.

- Do not shy away from bad news. Most volunteers will not complain to you about what they perceive to be small problems. Value the ones who do. Pay no attention to the gossips or the negative individuals who sometimes slip into a volunteer program, but acknowledge those individuals who have the courage to speak truth, no matter how unpleasant, when they perceive it to be for the greater good. You need people like this, because the sooner you are aware of a potential problem the sooner you can solve it. Do not forget to thank your bearer of bad news. That thank you will empower them to continue to be your extra pair of eyes needed to keep things running smoothly.

- Volunteers who want to grow need to learn to accept constructive criticism. Set a positive example for them. Demonstrate through your own actions and behavior how to receive criticism and work with the critic to turn their criticism into a constructive solution. Helping your volunteers learn how to do this is a truly empowering gift.

- Your attitude toward your volunteers is by and far the most effective tool you have for empowering them. Your faith in their ability to succeed will inspire and empower them. Nothing will buy you more loyalty from your volunteers than a positive, upbeat outlook that communicates your confidence that they are doing a good job.

CHAPTER 12:

WHEN PROBLEMS ARISE

A unique relationship is formed when a nonprofit accepts the services of a volunteer. Although the volunteer may perform duties that could be assigned to an employee, volunteers are not employees. A more accurate way to view them is as non-voting partners in your organization's mission. And, as any astute businessman or woman will tell you, one should never enter into a partnership without establishing an amicable way to dissolve the partnership if things do not work out. This is especially important when your partner is also — or has the potential to be — a donor. While a nonprofit should have a clearly defined policy for terminating a volunteer's service, every effort should be made to avoid having to use it.

Problems Are Inevitable

Most of the time, the partnership between you and your volunteers will function smoothly; you will benefit from your volunteer's services and your volunteer will achieve the personal goals that motivated him or her to volunteer. But people being

people, problems can arise: the incident may be triggered by a clash of personalities or a conflict over responsibilities. A well-meaning volunteer may misunderstand or inadvertently breach established policy. And no matter how conscientious you are in screening candidates, no process is 100 percent accurate. On occasion, a dysfunctional person has been known to slip in under the radar despite the best of intentions. Whatever the cause of your problem, you need to be prepared to address it. One disruptive volunteer left unchecked can disrupt even the best-run volunteer program.

Problems do not develop overnight, they evolve. An alert volunteer manager can usually spot the signs: a noticeable change in a volunteer's attitude or performance; an increase in volunteer-supervisor conflicts; or less laughter and more impatience among volunteers. Observation and a few questions will usually uncover the source of the problem.

When the evolving conflict is between two volunteers or a volunteer and a staff member, sometimes you can mediate a solution both can agree to. (See Chapter 8: Handling Staff-Volunteer Conflict.) But when the cause of the problem is the disruptive or inappropriate behavior of a volunteer, it must be addressed directly with the volunteer. The meeting should be private and confidential, between the volunteer manager or volunteer coordinator and the problem volunteer.

When Meeting with Your Problem Volunteer:

- Avoid accusatory language. You are there to seek a solution, not fix blame.

- Explain the reason for the meeting — the disruptive nature of the problem and the effect it is having on the other volunteers and your organization's mission.

- Allow the volunteer to present his or her perception of the situation without interruption.

- When the volunteer finishes presenting his or her side of the story, ask pertinent questions to clarify the information you now have.

- Express your appreciation for the service the volunteer has given to the organization and acknowledge you understand his or her commitment to its mission, but point out how the behavior in question is affecting other volunteers and negatively affecting the department's or unit's ability to accomplish its work.

- Invite the volunteer to help you find a solution to the problem.

- If it becomes clear the volunteer is a bad fit for the assignment and no longer wants to be there, try to find a graceful way to allow him or her to move on. The answer may be another assignment; it may be for the volunteer to take a leave of absence until he or she is ready to resume their commitment; or perhaps you might terminate their relationship with your organization. If the volunteer responds with belligerence, remain calm and suggest he or she consider some other program better suited to their needs and interests. Follow through by setting up an appointment for an exit interview.

- If the volunteer is cooperative and appears to want to work out the problem, confirm the suggestions you both agreed to and make two copies. You and the volunteer should sign both copies, one of which the volunteer will keep, the other for your files. Schedule a follow-up meeting in a week to ten days, or within an appropriate time span dictated by the volunteer's schedule, to revisit the problem and determine if it has been solved.

- Create a case file on the situation for your records.

The second meeting should be used to assess whether there has been a constructive change in attitude or behavior. Compliment the volunteer on his or her efforts. If indicated, you and the volunteer might agree on some other steps to improve the situation further.

If no progress has been made toward a solution, a new "contract" between you and the volunteer should be drawn up and signed, and a third meeting should be scheduled within the next ten days. If during this third meeting you determine that change has not and will not occur, it is time to terminate the volunteer's service with your organization.

A Reliable Behavior Guide and Exit Policy

Many problems can be prevented simply by providing volunteers with a handbook that clearly explains your organization's policies and what is considered unacceptable behavior. The handbook should also specify how any breach of appropriate conduct will be handled.

One organization that follows and endorses this concept is the Missoula Aging Services in western Montana. Curtis Hammond, the organization's volunteer coordinator, says this policy has proved to be beneficial to both his paid staff and his volunteers when problems arise.

Below is an excerpt from the Missoula Aging Services Volunteer Handbook explaining the organization's policy on misconduct and the dismissal of volunteers.

From Missoula Aging Services Handbook

TERMINATION

The decision to terminate your volunteer service is not taken lightly at Missoula Aging Services. The decision to terminate a volunteer will have careful forethought on the part of the supervisor. A written letter, documenting reason for termination, will be given to the volunteer. Volunteers have the right to appeal the decision to terminate through the appropriate grievance policy procedure.

TERMINATION FOR CAUSE

The following actions will result in termination of volunteer's services:

- Disregard for Confidentiality
- Discrimination
- Documented physical and/or verbal abuse of a client or staff
- Repeated absences without notification to supervisor
- Inappropriate conduct
- Theft
- Unwillingness to serve as scheduled

- Inability to carry out assigned duties because of poor health
- Inability to understand and follow directions
- Unwillingness or failure to attend mandatory training sessions
- Consuming alcoholic beverages during the performance of service activities

GRIEVANCE PROCEDURES

Any time a volunteer feels that he or she has been treated unfairly by a supervisor, the volunteer may request an interview with the appropriate program manager who will deal fairly and impartially with the situation. If a volunteer feels that he or she has been treated unfairly by the program manager, he or she may register a formal complaint with the executive director.

Appealing Termination

Any volunteer who has been terminated from a program may appeal this decision through the executive director. The executive director will fairly and impartially review any termination of volunteers.

Finding the Right Solutions

How you structure your policy for addressing problems will depend in part on the size and configuration of your organization and the nature of your mission. For example, larger organizations will have more opportunity to move their volunteers around, which gives them the option of solving problems by reassigning the volunteer or volunteers in question. This is a procedure favored by the Santa Fe Rape Crisis and Trauma Treatment Center:

Barbara Goldman, director emeritus, Santa Fe Rape Crisis and Trauma Treatment Center

"The Center's policy is based on the premise of an open door for volunteers and emphasis is placed on authentic, honest and 'whole' communication. We work for the best fit for our volunteers for each of our programs. When a difficulty arises, the supervisor, the executive director, and whomever else necessary, come together to resolve issues and, if necessary, to shift the volunteer to another program."

When an organization deals with a client population that is at risk, even a small breach of protocol can cause major problems. Sometimes all that is needed to ameliorate a problematic situation is a cool head and a conversation to clarify the issue. This was the approach Jane Lowe with the Winthrop P. Rockefeller Cancer Institute at UAMS took to solve a potentially dangerous situation created by a well-meaning volunteer:

Jane Lowe, volunteer coordinator, Winthrop P. Rockefeller Cancer Institute at UAMS

"A volunteer was showing up sometimes on a Saturday and Sunday when only the infusion center for Multiple Myeloma is open. (We are an outpatient facility.) She brought snacks…some homemade. The Multiple Myeloma patients must be extremely careful about what they eat and how it is prepared. I showed the volunteer the policy.

I also showed her the policy about letting the volunteer office know when she is planning to come when the office is closed so someone else on staff can be notified she will be there and can supervise her.

It was wonderful that she wanted to come on a weekend, and she understood the policy when it was explained. She now informs us when she is coming and if she brings snacks they are prepackaged… nothing out of her kitchen and we let the supervisor in charge know she will be there.

There are situations when talking with the volunteer proves fruitless and moving them is either not an option or would only result in transferring the problem from one department to another. In situations such as this, the only option left for the volunteer coordinator is to dismiss the volunteer. The process is never easy, and varies from situation to situation. Here are examples of how volunteer coordinators in three different types of nonprofits handled this challenge.

Marisa Albanese, volunteer coordinator, Union Station Homeless Services, Pasadena, California

"I had a situation where a volunteer needed to be dismissed because of inappropriate behavior with our clients. The manner in which I chose to handle the situation was to have the volunteer's supervisor dismiss the volunteer. Even though this was a bit uncomfortable for the staff member, I felt this was best because the volunteer most directly interacted with the supervisor on a weekly basis. I supported the supervisor's decision by being present at the meeting, but let her do the talking. I am comfortable with the results and feel if I would have dismissed the volunteer, the staff member would have needed to speak with him [the supervisor] as well."

Lori Tsuruda, volunteer coordinator, People Making a Difference (PMD)

People Making a Difference organizes one-time, hands-on volunteer projects that engage individuals and partners with businesses to promote effective community involvement, and trains and assists nonprofit leaders in improving volunteer management in New England. Despite the low threshold of commitment (three to seven hours), we have had people unable to participate reliably within our parameters for cancellations, on-time arrivals and departures, and conduct policies. When a grievous infraction occurs we follow up by explaining the situation and giving a warning, then remind them of the requirements the next time they sign up to participate in a PMD service project. If the infraction occurs again, we express our sadness that they are currently unable to participate in our service program and we remove them from our lists. We are comfortable with the results since we consistently hold all of our volunteers to the same standards."

"Firing" a volunteer is probably the most difficult task you will do as a volunteer manager or coordinator. It is never a pleasant experience, but one of your primary responsibilities is to ensure your volunteers and staff a safe and congenial work environment. This means an environment free of disruptive or destructive individuals whose behavior creates discord.

The question becomes not whether you should dismiss the problematic volunteer, but how you can carry out this responsibility in a way that creates as little collateral damage as possible.

Limiting Collateral Damage

Many dynamics are activated when you "fire" a volunteer: The volunteer's feeling of rejection or anger; your suppressed feelings of anger at being forced into this situation; the impact of the dismissal on the volunteer's friends and other volunteers. You cannot

change the situation, but the way you handle the termination may enable you to avoid collateral damage.

> "There is just one way to fire someone: with love and support and deep, deep regret. You must try as much as possible to make the act itself a caring confrontation."
>
> — James A. Autry, *Love and Profit: The Art of Caring Leadership*

By collateral damage we are speaking of the repercussions that could occur from firing the volunteer. Will the individual be so angry he or she might seek retribution by destroying property or attacking whomever he or she feels is responsible for the humiliation? Will they lash out at your organization in public or private in a way that could damage your brand? Will dismissing the volunteer have a negative impact on the friends the volunteer has made in the program or on volunteer morale? Are there any legal ramifications to your actions that you need to be aware of? (This may depend on state laws.) While these concerns may seem extreme, they are not without precedent. It is, therefore, in your best interest and the best interest of your organization to make the dismissal process as non-confrontational as possible. Here are some suggestions:

- Do not discuss your decision to terminate the volunteer's services with other volunteers or staff, with the possible exception of the volunteer's supervisor if this individual has been involved in the decision.

- Meet with the volunteer in a private place where you will not be disturbed.

- Arrange to have a third party present as a witness so the individual being terminated cannot misrepresent what takes place. The third party should preferably be of the same sex as the employee being terminated to avoid accusations of sexual harassment.

- You may be harboring some anger over the situation. Leave it at the door. Maintain a professional demeanor. Know what you are going to say in advance. Rehearse it if necessary.

- Be civil, but keep your conversation to a minimum. You

are not there to try to rectify the situation, only to bring about closure. Stay focused.

- The volunteer is likely to perceive your decision as a sign you have little or no regard for his or her time or talents, which were offered so generously to your organization. Rejection is a painful emotion. While you know your actions are right and necessary, show some compassion for the individual's pain.

- Prepare two copies of a statement recounting the reasons for the termination, your organization's policy for termination, and the volunteer's agreement to leave. Read the statement to the volunteer. If he or she agrees the document is accurate, you and the volunteer will sign both copies. You may also want your witness to sign the document. You will give one copy to the volunteer and keep the other for your files.

- Collect any keys, badges, uniforms, or any other items connected with the program your volunteer has used to gain access to the area or identifies him or her as volunteer for your organization.

- Thank the volunteer for past services. Express your regret things did not work out. Be sincere. Wish the volunteer luck.

- If appropriate, leave the door open for the volunteer to be considered at another time for another type of involvement with the organization.

- To avoid rumors or misunderstandings, inform any friends the volunteer had in the program or volunteers the individual worked with that he or she will not be coming back. Do not go into detail. When asked why, a simple "For personal reasons" will suffice.

"Poor performance by even one volunteer can reinforce negative attitudes about volunteers among paid staff who are negative or ambivalent about engaging volunteers. Paid staff may become hesitant to request volunteers or refuse to design opportunities for volunteers within the organization."

— Mary V. Merrill, Supervising Volunteers

Your job is not finished with dismissing the troublesome volunteer. You need to check to see if this individual has left any problems behind. If the dismissed volunteer had clashes with staff or other volunteers, is there any residual hurt or suppressed anger that needs to be addressed? Ignored, these problems could cost you another volunteer or sabotage the good volunteer-employee relationships you have worked so hard to build. Seek out anyone who was involved with the dismissed employee and inquire if they are all right. Give them an opportunity to get the hurt or anger out so they can go on to enjoy the comfortable, rewarding volunteer experience they hoped to find in your organization.

Some Tips for Handling Volunteer-Related Problems

- Your relationship with your volunteers is a partnership. Make sure you have a workable mechanism in place that will enable you to dissolve this partnership amicably if things do not work out.

- Many volunteer-related problems can be avoided by clarifying acceptable and unacceptable conduct in your volunteer handbook.

- Everything should be done to retain a volunteer before making the decision to terminate their relationship with the organization. Once that decision is made, the volunteer coordinator should work to make the meetings with the troublesome volunteer as non-confrontational as possible.

- Volunteers tend to be busy people. Even if they take the time to read your policy statements, they may not retain the details. To avoid future problems, especially with volunteers who deal directly with an agency's clients, it is a good idea to hold periodic meetings with volunteers to go over important policies that affect their work.

- Here is an idea for organizations that work with the elderly or people with serious medical problems that place restrictions on their activities or diet: do not rely on your volunteers reading and retaining information you provide related to these restrictions. Consider having a doctor or a nurse address one of your volunteer meetings to explain and answer questions about the special precautions that must be observed with this population. Whether the meeting is mandatory or voluntary, serve some refreshments and find some way to make it fun. If it is a pleasant experience for your volunteers and not just an information session, they will be more likely to remember the information.

- For your legal protection, and the protection of your organization, always have a witness present when you confront a problematic volunteer privately to verify what is being said and agreed upon.

- It is sound policy to detail in writing the offenses or breach of good conduct that created a need for the meeting between you and a problematic volunteer. Once the accuracy of the document is confirmed it should be signed by the volunteer coordinator, the volunteer in question, and the witness. One copy should be given to the volunteer and one should be retained by the volunteer coordinator for his or her files.

- To avoid accusations of sexual harassment, the witness asked to attend any meetings between the volunteer coordinator and a difficult volunteer should be of the same sex as the volunteer.

- The best time to solve a problem is before it becomes full blown. Keep an eye out for subtle changes: signs of discontentment, a decrease in a volunteer's performance level, or a shift in your volunteer team's mood — less laughter and more flaring up of tempers.

- You may see the first signs of an impending problem not in the actions of the perpetrator, but in the impact his or her harassment or insensitive behavior is having on the victim. If you suspect something is wrong, do not wait. Ask questions and get to the root of the problem as quickly as possible.

- When a volunteer's behavior leaves no other option than "firing" him or her, if the volunteer's supervisor has been part of the decision, consider letting the supervisor do the actual firing or at least include him or her as an active part of the process. The supervisor was the individual who most directly interacted with the volunteer and is most knowledgeable about the issue that triggered the dismissal. It is always good policy to let the person bringing the complaint and the person being terminated because of the complaint to reconcile the problem face to face. This leaves no room for rumor or misconceptions.

- When discussing a problem with a volunteer, focus on performance or behavior and avoid personal issues or value comments.

- When conducting an exit interview, be sure to collect any keys, name tags, badges, or other work-related items before you conclude the meeting.

- It is normal to feel nervous when confronting a difficult volunteer, especially if you know that confrontation is going to end in firing that volunteer. Some people react to nervousness by talking excessively. Avoid this. It could lead to confusion or send the wrong message to the volunteer. Be civil, but keep your conversation brief and to the point and stay focused.

- Some people find writing down what they are going to say and rehearsing it ahead of time makes meetings with difficult volunteers less stressful.

- Boorish or inappropriate volunteer behavior should not be tolerated. It can drive good, productive volunteers away.

- Documentation is important when dealing with the dismissal of a volunteer. Everything, from the first complaint to the final exit interview, should be documented to protect the volunteer coordinator and the organization in case the dismissed volunteer files a complaint or institutes legal action over the issue.

- Volunteer evaluation provides volunteer coordinators with an effective means to avoid or defuse potential problems. The consistent monitoring of a volunteer's performance alerts the volunteer coordinator of negative changes in the volunteer's performance or attitude. The routine meetings also provide an opportunity for volunteers to discuss situations in the workplace that disturb or concern them.

- Maintaining an open door policy and encouraging feedback from volunteers and staff enables a volunteer coordinator to keep his or her finger on the pulse of the program. If volunteers and staff are made to feel comfortable bringing their concerns to the volunteer coordinator, there is less of a chance small offenses or affronts will be internalized and fester into major confrontations. If they are aware of a pending problem early, the volunteer coordinator has the chance to address it before it becomes a serious problem.

- Interpersonal problems can arise when your volunteers form cliques. Instead of a culture of inclusion, you end up with a culture of "them" and "us." Team building is one way to solve this problem. Another way is to promote inclusion in job assignments. You can also address the problem directly by asking volunteers in the "in group" to help make excluded volunteers feel welcome. Often the exclusion is not intentional; it is the result of the tendency people have to gravitate to people they know and with whom they feel comfortable.

- While writing a positive letter of recommendation for a dismissed volunteer may ease the volunteer coordinator's sense of guilt for having had to fire the volunteer, it is a bad practice that in the end simply creates problems for another volunteer coordinator at another nonprofit.

- When dealing with minor infractions, the volunteer coordinator should look at the volunteer's misstep as a teaching opportunity. For example, if the volunteer, intending only to be helpful, puts a client in jeopardy with his or her actions, point out to the volunteer the possible problems he or she might have caused and use the incident to reinforce the critical importance of following procedure when dealing with clients.

- Firing a volunteer should be done thoughtfully, for cause — a logical decision based on irrefutable facts. Never fire someone when you are angry or upset without having carefully worked through the grievances with which the volunteer has been charged.

- No matter how sound your reason is for dismissing a volunteer, do so with empathy. As Sarah Jane Rehnborg, Ph.D., associate director of the RGK Center for Philanthropy and Community Service at the University of Texas in Austin and an authority on volunteer management reminds us "Firing a volunteer is tantamount to telling the person that the 'gift' of him or herself made to your organization is neither sufficient nor worthy."

- The ability to solve problems and, when necessary, dismiss disruptive volunteers with a minimum of collateral damage are skills that are as important for a volunteer coordinator to have as the ability to motivate and inspire volunteers. For volunteers to thrive in a nonprofit, they must be confident the organization will provide a safe and nurturing environment in which they can pursue personal growth and develop and share their gifts.

CHAPTER 13:

UNDERSTANDING AND SUCCESSFULLY USING MOTIVATION

We live in a culture that is always looking for a quick fix. Want to motivate your volunteers? Give them an award, throw a party, or provide a challenge. All of these are legitimate volunteer motivators, but an organization that wants to encourage long-term volunteer commitment needs more than a bag of motivational ideas. To accomplish its goal, the need to motivate volunteers must inform all of an organization's policies and decisions; it must be as much a part of the organization's mission as the work it is committed to do.

"Treat people as if they were what they ought to be, and help them become what they are capable of being."

— Johann von Goethe (1749 – 1832), German writer and philosopher

This concept requires a shift in the way most nonprofits view themselves. Nonprofits tend to see their mission as their raison d'être — their reason for existing — but there is another equally important reason for nonprofits to exist: the role they play in providing people with an opportunity to share their gifts, talents, and treasure for the good of others. Providing this opportunity is as valuable to society as feeding the hungry, housing the homeless, or healing the sick. Once an organization makes this slight adjustment to its thinking, motivating volunteers becomes a rewarding adventure instead of a burdensome task.

The "To" and "Who" of Motivation

The word "motivation" tends to be bandied around as if it had a universal meaning. In reality it has no meaning unless it is followed by the word "to." We do not simply motivate people; we motivate them to do something. Both the type of person we are trying to motivate and what it is we are trying to motivate them to do will determine the appropriate motivational tool or approach we will need to use.

Let us consider the "to" first. If your goal is simply to motivate your volunteers to show up, all you have to do is make their onsite experience comfortable and fun. If you want to motivate them to accomplish something, you still need to make their experience comfortable and fun, but you would also want to employ motivators such as establishing a realistic goal for them or the promise of some kind of reward or recognition when the project is completed.

For the sake of argument, let us assume everyone reading this book wants their volunteers to do more than just show up: they want to motivate them to make a long-term commitment. This requires a comprehensive strategy. The best place to begin is by understanding who your volunteers are and how they think. Fortunately, there is a tool available to help determine this — the DiSC model of human behavior.

The DiSC Model of Human Behavior

We all have a distinct way of thinking, feeling, and acting that determines our behavioral style. This is the idea behind the four-quadrant DiSC model of human behavior. The model helps to provide insight into why people do what they do based on their behavioral styles and behavioral preferences. *DiSC was developed by Dr. William Moulton Marston at Columbia University in 1928, and was later updated by Dr. John Geier and Inscape Publishing at the University of Minnesota.* The acronym refers to what the model identifies as the four categories of human behavior style: **D**ominance, **I**nfluence, **S**tability (Submission), and **C**onscientiousness (Compliance). According to this model, each of these behavior styles has effective and ineffective traits. See if you recognize any of your volunteers in the list below.

Why is the "i" in DiSC written with a lower case letter?

Good question! Nobody is completely sure where it came from. Some say that there was a typo in the original printed materials, and not enough money to reprint. Others say it's a trademark, or just to be quirky and catch your attention.

DOMINANCE

Volunteers who fall into this category are direct, self-assured, and capable of getting quick results. On the negative side, they can be dictatorial, demanding, and sarcastic.

INFLUENCE

Volunteers who fall into this category are people-oriented and persuasive. They like to be in the center of things and contribute their thoughts or ideas. However, they can also have a tendency to talk too much and sometimes they have difficulty maintaining focus.

STABILITY

Originally called Submission by Dr. Marston, this category encompasses volunteers who are loyal, consistent, and good listeners. They can also be indecisive and resistant to change.

CONSCIENTIOUSNESS

Originally labeled Compliance by Dr. Marston, volunteers in this category are detail oriented and can usually be relied on for accuracy. On the negative side, they can also be perfectionists or overly critical.

For convenience, we will refer to the four types as type D, type I, type S, and type C.

A brief anecdote points out the value of understanding these behavior styles: Some years ago, I worked with a community theater in Washington State. The small community had taken the theater to its heart and attracting capable volunteers was no problem — retaining them was. I inadvertently discovered a clue to the reason one evening as the volunteers were preparing the house for a performance.

An angry voice caught my attention. One of the volunteers was complaining loudly to his wife. The man had been a successful accountant and was now retired. He had been studying the theater's box office procedure and had come up with an idea on how to make the process more efficient. In his enthusiasm, he had decided not to wait, but tell the volunteer coordinator about his idea that evening.

In defense of the volunteer coordinator, it was opening night and things were hectic. When the volunteer tried to present his idea, the volunteer coordinator brusquely cut him off saying there was nothing wrong with the system they had; it worked perfectly well. Then she loaded him down with boxes of programs and in explicit detail proceeded to explain to him precisely how they should be distributed.

It would have been more prudent to suggest to him that they discuss his idea at a more opportune time. Rebuffing him as she did dealt a blow to his self-esteem. However, what angered the man even more was what he perceived to be the condescending manner in which she had instructed him on how to distribute the programs. "She treated me as if I were senile," he told his wife, "like I didn't have the brains to hand out a stupid program!"

Had this situation occurred with an S type there would probably have been no repercussions. A detail-oriented C type might even have appreciated such explicit instructions. But the volunteer coordinator was dealing with a D type who took offence at the disrespectful way he felt he was being treated.

If the volunteer coordinator had been aware of the DiSC model, she might have recognized the volunteer as a D type and probably would have handled the situation differently to avoid alienating him. Her lack of knowledge cost her a capable volunteer.

Knowing whom you are trying to motivate is crucial if you want to be sure you are using the right approach and the right motivational tools to achieve your goal.

Tips for Motivating D Type Volunteers (Dominance)

- Be sensitive to their ego, respectful of their time, and appreciative of their efforts.

- Annual reports and overviews of your organization's operation that provide insight into your stewardship are strong motivators for this type of volunteer.

- Understand they have little patience with small talk. When giving them instruction or information, keep in mind they appreciate clarity and brevity.

- To empower them, give them an opportunity to initiate action or submit ideas. Provide assignments with quick solutions. They work best on the conceptual level and prefer to delegate the details to someone else.

- When providing them with feedback, always be candid and specific.

- Make them aware you recognize their talents and skills by providing ways to employ them.

- Keep challenging them.

- They take achievement seriously and prefer to have their achievements acknowledged or rewarded formally. They are usually motivated by the possibility of getting a plaque or some handsome award they can display in their office or home.

- When possible, place them with other high achievers — other D types and C types. They should do well with assistance from S types, but probably not with I types.

- Often this type of individual volunteers to accomplish something specific. Find out what it is they want to accomplish and do your best to help them achieve this personal goal.

Tips for Motivating I Type Volunteers (Influence)

- Social interaction is a major motivator for I type volunteers. Place them in assignments where they will be working with other people.

- Provide them with an opportunity to use their persuasive skills with assignments such as finding in-kind donations, raising funds, promoting events, or making presentations about your organization.

- They often do well working with clients as long as there are professionals on hand to supervise and maintain boundaries.

- Avoid assignments that will isolate them or require them to focus heavily on details.

- Involve them in celebratory events, award programs, and recognition events.

- In rewarding or recognizing their accomplishments, focus more on fun than formality.

- Publicize their volunteer achievements beyond your organization. Make their accomplishments known in their myriad of social circles.

- They frequently enjoy such things as bringing in home-baked cookies or other refreshments and hosting volunteer-related events in their home. Provide the opportunity for them to engage in these types of activities, and acknowledge the value of these contributions.

- They enjoy taking part in events outside of work that bring volunteers together in social interaction. Involve them in the planning and executing of these types of events.

- An attractive, cheerful milieu where people are friendly and laughter is welcome will help to bring this type of volunteer back again and again.

Tips for Motivating S Type Volunteers (Stability)

- Your story — the history of your organization, how you are pursuing your mission, and the role you play in the community — are strong motivators for these volunteers who believe loyalty to be a virtue, and seek good causes that will enable them to practice this virtue.

- Your recognition and gratitude for their loyalty helps to motivate continued service, but displays of recognition and appreciation should be kept low-key. These volunteer are usually made uncomfortable by too much attention.

- They are most comfortable with assignments that provide routine and consistency.

- Change makes them uncomfortable. If change is required, these volunteers adapt more easily to it if it is made in increments instead of all at once.

- They work well paired with a D type volunteers or staff member for whom they can provide consistent, loyal support, or with a C type who knows how to give instructions and appreciates someone who can follow them with consistency.

- Because they prefer to avoid the spotlight, motivate them by giving them a strong supportive role and praise them for being the solid foundation on which the event or activity has been constructed.

- Their listening skills make them well suited to work with clients recovering from trauma or needing someone to hear them, and they are empowered by this kind of interaction.

- Challenge may not be a motivator for them because of the discomfort they feel with change.

- Placing them in assignments that require them to make decisions could stress them.

- They prefer assignments in which they can display their ability to meticulously follow directions.

Tips for Motivating C Type Volunteers (Conscientiousness)

- These volunteers are best motivated by assignments that appeal to their proclivity for detail and accuracy. They are most comfortable following procedures and standards. Record keeping, maintaining a budget, and proof reading are all good possibilities.

- These volunteers usually make excellent candidates to help office staff, unless the staff is disorganized or slipshod. If the staff is comfortable with them organizing the office, the challenge would be motivating. If the staff resists organizing efforts, the assignment would drive these volunteers away.

- The most motivating parts of your story for these volunteers are the details demonstrating your excellent stewardship and the successful numbers your organization is able to show for your work. (Number of people helped, number of wells installed, or number of lives saved for example.)

- These volunteers respond well to challenge if the challenge addresses their passion for accuracy and detail. They would be motivated by an opportunity to help improve your bookkeeping or filling system, or the chance to help you save money by finding errors or waste that can be eliminated from your program. Given such opportunities, they will thrive in your organization.

- They prefer to work alone without distraction.

- If you do give them an assignment that requires working with others, they work better with a D type volunteer or staff member than with an I or S type.

- They may enjoy some social interaction that does not distract from their work, but they are not motivated by it, and in some cases lack patience for this aspect of volunteering.

- They prefer to be rewarded for results, rather than effort.

- In training these volunteers, you will want to present proof and facts and be equipped to answer questions.

- They do not trust easily. They tend to harbor suspicion until they have enough evidence of the legitimacy of an organization. But once you succeed in gaining their trust, you have loyal, capable supporters eager to give you their best.

If you are interested in learning more about DiSC or would like to explore some of the management programs that show you how to apply the DiSC model, you can use an internet search to look up the term for a list of companies that provide these programs. For the purpose of managing volunteers, becoming aware of the four types of volunteers, and what motivates each one, can help you be more effective in dealing with and motivating your volunteers; however, the primary reason the DiSC model has been included here is as a reminder that volunteers are not a homogeneous group. They cannot be motivated by a one-size-fits-all approach. Every volunteer is different, and will respond best to motivational efforts that resonate with his or her individual nature and interests. This is what makes motivating volunteers not just a skill, but an art.

The Job as a Motivator

In some instances, the motivational efforts of the volunteer manager or the organization pales next to the power of the volunteer assignment to motivate deep commitment in a volunteer. Case in point: The hospital auxiliary program of the Winthrop P. Rockefeller Cancer Institute at the University of Arkansas for Medical Sciences in Little Rock, Arkansas, the area's only comprehensive cancer facility. On average, more than 10,700 patient visits are recorded each month. Here is a report from Jane Lowe, director of the institute's volunteer services and Auxiliary.

VOLUNTEER STORIES FROM THE FIELD

Winthrop P. Rockefeller Cancer Institute at UAMS
Little Rock, Arkansas
http://cancer.uams.edu/volunteer

The mission of the Cancer Institute's Auxiliary is to provide information, service, compassion, and hope to those whose lives are touched by cancer. The department has six paid staff members and 500 volunteers who work in waiting rooms, offices, and serve as "wayfinders" and escorts for new patients. They also work in the Auxiliary gift shop and on two large fundraisers.

Report from Jane Lowe, CVM, director, Volunteer Services/ Auxiliary/Gift shop

Our 11-story building is outpatient so our patients are here every day. They are our guests and our customers. I am always amazed, gratified, and inspired by the way our volunteers are so dedicated and are willing to go above and beyond to make sure the patients in the waiting rooms are comfortable and not in need of anything. It makes such a difference to the volunteers to see the same patients each time they are here to do a shift so they actually get to know them.

Although volunteers cannot replace paid staff, the things they do are invaluable. The staff really doesn't know what they would do without their assistance with the patients. Because our patients may be here for weeks or months, the volunteers can really make friends with them. We have a knitting group and the patients, caregivers, and the volunteers love it. The smiles, greetings, and visiting the volunteers do with the patients make them feel more comfortable and a little more at home, especially those from out of state or out of the country. The volunteers have wonderful stories to tell. I know we are making a difference, and I know that my volunteers are happy here.

While the sense of fulfillment the volunteers involved in the institute's Auxiliary get from working with the patients is unquestionably their greatest motivator to keep volunteering, there are other factors at work here that help to make their volunteer experience pleasurable.

The Auxiliary has volunteer appreciation luncheons that are usually held at volunteer's homes away from the Institute's campus. "The volunteers love the camaraderie and getting to be with each other," Lowe says.

Lowe also provides treats for the volunteers in the Auxiliary's office, where Auxiliary members are invited to spend their breaks or come for a snack. Volunteers are also given lunch tickets on the days they work so they can go to lunch together.

Training is also used to motivate the Auxiliary's volunteers to deepen their commitment. It is even better if you can make the training fun. "Our in-services are always fun," Lowe says, "with skits and power points that entertain while they teach."

On occasion Lowe supplements her in-service programs with special training events. After reading *If Disney Ran Your Hospital: 9 ½ Things You Would Do Differently* by Fred Lee, she arranged for the entire hospital staff and all the volunteers to participate in the Disney Initiative Customer Service Training, conducted by the Walt Disney Organization. All the volunteers were required to attend. "Some balked a little," Lowe says, "but they were all so happy they had attended and it made them feel more responsible and more a part of the campus."

What does an effective motivational strategy for a nonprofit look like? It looks like the program we have just discussed. It has:

- An institutional philosophy in which the importance of keeping volunteers motivated informs all policy and decisions.

- A range of volunteer assignments that engage, challenge, and provide a sense of fulfillment for various types of volunteers.

- A working environment that is welcoming and comfortable.

- A way to recognize the value of volunteers that also provides an opportunity for socializing.

- A training program that empowers with knowledge while providing an experience that is fun.

This is the type of institutional vision and the kinds of motivation tools that, when used together, can successfully motivate volunteers to commit to a long-term relationship with an organization.

Some Tips to Help You Motivate Your Volunteers to Stay

- The need to motivate volunteers should be a part of a nonprofit's mission. It should inform all of the nonprofit's policies and decisions.

- Understanding your volunteers are not a homogenous group but individuals with different temperaments and needs is critical to understanding how to motivate them.

- Individuals develop distinct ways of thinking, feeling, and acting that becomes their behavioral style. The DiSC model of human behavior can help volunteer coordinators identify the behavioral style of their volunteers so they can target them with the appropriate kind of motivation to help them succeed and encourage them to make a long-term commitment to their organization.

- An achievement-motivated volunteer will be more successful in assignments that provide them with an opportunity to excel and quickly be bored by assignments where challenge is missing.

- Some volunteers are motivated by a need for recognition. Find projects for them that can be completed quickly and will put them in the spotlight. They tend to thrive in assignments that let them carry the agency's story into the community such as speaking at religious or civic organizations, dealing with the media, or recruiting new volunteers.

- Reimburse your volunteers for assignment-related expenses so being able to afford to volunteer never becomes an issue.

- Let your volunteers know you trust them by enlisting them as mentors for new volunteers.

- Provide on-going training so a volunteer who wants to take on a new challenge can always get the training they need before moving into a new job. This also enables a volunteer to test out a new kind of work before making a commitment.

- Provide opportunities, and scholarships if possible, for volunteers to attend conferences or workshops that will help them expand their skills.

- Occasionally bring in special training programs. If you are affiliated with an association that offers workshops that would benefit your volunteers, arrange to have your volunteers attend some of these workshops. Investing in your volunteers in this manner builds loyalty and enthusiasm for your organization.

- Stay tuned in to your volunteers' lives. Offer to call or provide a letter of recommendation if you discover your volunteer is being considered for a new job or if a younger volunteer has applied to a college.

- Provide visual proof of your commitment to your volunteers: A plaque prominently displayed in your offices recognizing volunteers who have been involved for a number of years; a framed picture of your "Volunteer of the Month" in the lobby; annual group photos of all your volunteers or teams of volunteers displayed in the hallways.

- An idea from Volunteer Canada: gift wrap votive candles with a note saying "You light up the lives of so many," and give them to volunteers to remind them, regardless of their assignment, they are a part of a mission that is doing good.

- Post laminated copies of thank you notes from clients where they can be seen by volunteers and guests.

- Randomly send small gifts of appreciation and thank you letters to volunteers to let them know they are appreciated.

- If a story appears in local newspapers about a volunteer, post the story, and frame a copy of it to give to the volunteer.

- Assign a volunteer with photography skills to take pictures of your volunteers at work. Matte and frame the pictures with a thank you message and give the pictures to the volunteer as a holiday gift, or as part of a recognition ceremony or another event.

- Do you have a mundane chore that needs to be done? Want to motivate volunteers to chip in? Add food. The Santa Fe Symphony gets mailings out by hosting volunteers in a private home with the promise of a pot of soup and good company.

- If you want to motivate someone to do something again, be sure to show your appreciation for their efforts. Here is another idea from Volunteer Canada for showing appreciation to volunteers involved in fundraising that is guaranteed to get a smile: Place a strip of magnetic tape on the back of a small box of raisins and add a note saying "Thanks for raisin' all those funds." Recipients can display this whimsical token of your appreciation on their refrigerators or a metal filing cabinet at work.

- Responsibility is always a motivator for volunteers. The key to making it work is to know your volunteer well enough to understand what kind and how much responsibility will motivate them without stressing them. Using the DiSC model, a D type volunteer will be motivated by responsibility for developing a concept to improve an organization's operation, but not the responsibility of handling the details to carry it out. An I type volunteer will thrive given responsibility for taking the stage to promote your organization, but quickly become disenchanted if the task requires him or her to juggle the details of making all the arrangements. A C type volunteer will relish the responsibility to peruse your books for errors or ways to save money, but do not ask them to make a report on their findings in front of a large audience. An S type volunteer will responsibly handle an assignment working with clients, as long as they have a pattern to follow and do not have to make important decisions. Challenge your volunteers with responsibility, but choose the responsibility carefully.

- Do not just instruct, but collaborate with your volunteers. Show them you respect and appreciate them. Solicit their opinions and invite their suggestions. And when their ideas or suggestions prove workable, make sure you let them know.

- Volunteer work is by nature task oriented and departmentalized. To keep your volunteers motivated you need to constantly sell them on the big picture — the overall mission you are all working to accomplish. And you need to keep them anchored in the context of the mission so they never lose the sense they are playing an important role in accomplishing it.

- If you hear no laughter coming from your volunteers, you are not doing your job well. As soon as volunteering ceases to be fun, the volunteer ceases to volunteer.

- Motivating volunteers to make long-term commitments is not just the job of the volunteer coordinator. It takes the cooperation of the board, the executive director, the staff and other volunteers.

- Your volunteers are motivated by every interaction you have with them. The trick is to motivate them to stay, not to go.

CHAPTER 14:

VOLUNTEERS AND FUNDRAISING

Fundraising is not just another activity for a nonprofit; it is *the* activity that makes it possible for the nonprofit to exist. Considering how crucial it is for survival, one would expect nonprofits to use every possible resource they have in their quest for funding. Yet there is a mindset among some not-for-profit organizations that, with the exception of those volunteers who have been recruited specifically for fundraising, volunteers and fundraising are not a good mix. The misconceptions seem to evolve from a fear that any effort they make to involve their volunteers in fundraising would jeopardize their relationship with them. The opposite is true. While incorporating volunteers into your fundraising strategy requires some effort and a little imagination, no opportunity you can give them will deepen their understanding and commitment to your organization more powerfully.

Small community-based nonprofits with limited or no professional staff are, out of necessity, more likely to call upon their volunteers to do double duty, looking to them to provide both mission related and fundraising assistance. While the information that follows is directed to larger nonprofit organizations in which these two functions are more likely to be separated, smaller nonprofits may find some of the ideas and suggestions can be adapted to their programs as well.

Before you take steps to incorporate your non-fundraising volunteers into your fundraising efforts, you need to make sure your organization is ready to support your volunteers in this new role.

It All Begins with Your Volunteer Board of Directors

Ask any successful nonprofit what they look for when recruiting their volunteer board and you will hear the words "affluence" and "influence." They seek individuals who are in a position to give substantially to the organization, and/or who are well connected in the community and capable of attracting large personal and corporate contributions. Wisdom, integrity, and an abiding commitment to the organization's mission are also essential attributes in a candidate.

"Too often I have been engaged as a consultant only to have the executive director of the organization or chair of the board of trustees tell me, 'Our board doesn't raise money. You'll have to look elsewhere for fund-raising leadership.' That's when I tell them they need to change the makeup of the board."

— Tony Poderis, Fundraising Consultant

Accepting an appointment to the board of a nonprofit is a serious commitment. Board members assume legal and administrative responsibilities; they set policies and agendas; and they become the guardians of the organization's brand. Their most important responsibility is, or at least should be, fundraising.

Without the access to the community only a strong, well-connected, and dedicated board can provide, even professional fundraising consultants will be hard pressed to help a nonprofit raise sufficient funds to keep its mission going. You depend on your board to help plan your fundraising campaign, decide whether to engage professional help, and open the doors to many of your most important potential donors.

Your board will also play a key role if you decide to expand the structure of your capital campaign to include all your volunteers. You will need their support to institute this new approach and you will need their experience and savvy about fundraising to help you educate and inspire your volunteers who lack fundraising experience — the volunteers who are going to form the new support teams for your trained fund raisers.

Transforming Volunteers into Fundraising Support Teams

Annual capital campaigns and other fundraising efforts are frequently treated as if they were entities on to themselves. As a result, volunteers not directly connected with the campaign tend to see it as unrelated to their day-to-day involvement with the nonprofit — an activity out of the sphere of their responsibilities. The first step in building your fundraising support teams is to change that perception. You need to make

286 | 365 Ideas for Recruiting, Retaining, Motivating and Rewarding Your Volunteers

your fundraising campaign relevant to these volunteers. The most effective way to accomplish this is to include them.

STEP 1 – HOLD A MEETING

While your fundraising campaign is still in the conceptual stage, invite all your volunteers to a meeting and announce your plans. Board members involved in the planning, your fundraising coordinator, your volunteer manager, and your fundraising consultant — if you have one — should all participate in the presentation.

Here are some suggestions for the meeting agenda:

- Explain the reason for the campaign: what you are hoping to accomplish, why you need the money, and what you are planning to do with it. The more specific you can be the more effective your presentation will be. If you can, tie your goals to the work your volunteers are doing.

- For greater impact, employ visuals: charts, video, or pictures of volunteers working with clients; testimonials from experts about the need for more research; statements from clients who have been helped or from case workers explaining the need to expand services — whatever characterizes and personalizes why you need to raise money. Make sure your facts are accurate and keep your stories poignant. Your goal is to generate excitement and a sense of urgency so your volunteers will care about the upcoming campaign and want to help.

- Share the strategy you are planning to use to obtain your funds with your volunteers.

- Ask your volunteers for any ideas they might have for

improving your strategy — any suggestions they might have for other activities or ways to reach possible donors. Acknowledge viable ideas and include them in your strategy.

- Have a sign-up sheet available. Explain that now that they have given you their input, you are going to finalize the strategy. This will include establishing volunteer teams to support the fundraising campaign. Invite all volunteers interested in working on the campaign to sign up to receive a list of the teams so they can select how they would like to help.

- Thank everyone who signs up, and confirm they will be contacted as soon as a list of teams is available.

STEP 2 – DESIGN YOUR SUPPORT TEAMS

This step should be taken as quickly as possible after the initial meeting to take advantage of the enthusiasm you have built for the campaign. The types of teams you create will depend on the nature of your organization and the makeup of your corps of volunteers. The teams should be designed by the volunteer coordinator, in conjunction with the campaign coordinator. Together they understand both the talent available and the work that needs to be done. Here are some ideas to help you design your teams:

- **Form a social networking team:** Invite volunteers with a Digg, Facebook, Twitter, or any other social-networking account to form a team to help develop an appropriate OSN message about the campaign. Ask these volunteers to post the message on their OSN or OPN page. Some OSNs and OPNs have special pages where members can solicit donations for charities of their choice. These pages can provide another way to spread word about your campaign and invite people to donate.

- Your social networking team should be supervised by the campaign coordinator or someone well-versed in campaign policy to ensure the material they create is consistent with all the other campaign-related material being disseminated.

- Team members should take responsibility for tracking the responses to their messages; they should meet periodically during the campaign to report these responses, and to tweak the message if necessary. If leads are received, suggesting a possible large donation, they should be turned over to a trained fund raiser for follow-up.

- **Form a blogging team**: This team should be made up of bloggers and, with appropriate supervision, should be charged with creating fundraising material for use by volunteers who like to blog. Pattern the team's operational procedure after the one described above for the social networking team.

- **Form an email team:** This team will help create an email or series of email messages that persuasively invite the recipient to join the campaign by making a donation. Each member of the team will provide 15 or more names from their email address book to receive the message. While the recipient will respond to the organization so a credit card can be used for the donation, the volunteer who provided the name will be referenced for credibility.

The Nine Basic Truths of Fundraising

By Tony Poderis

Basic Truth #1: Organizations are not entitled to support; they must earn it.

Basic Truth #2: Successful fundraising is not magic; it is simply hard work on the part of people who are thoroughly prepared.

Basic Truth #3: Fundraising is not raising funds; it is raising friends.

Basic Truth # 4: You do not raise money by begging for it; you raise it by selling people on your organization.

Basic Truth #5: People do not just reach for their checkbooks and give money to an organization; they have to be asked to give.

Basic Truth #6: You do not wait for the "right" moment to ask; you ask now.

Basic Truth #7: Successful fundraising officers do not ask for the money; they get others to ask for it — someone in the prospect's peer group.

Basic Truth #8: You do not decide today to ask for it tomorrow; it takes time, patience, and planning.

Basic Truth #9: Prospects and donors are not cash crops waiting to be harvested; treat them as you would customers in a business.

It does not take a genius to raise money. The process is a combination of common sense, hard work, preparation, courtesy, commitment, enthusiasm, understanding, and a belief in what you are asking others to support.

- The recipient should also be offered an alternative: a phone number they can call if they have questions or would rather make their donation over the phone. If the organization has any fundraising events coming up, this information should be included in the email. By forming an email team instead of just asking for names, you involve the volunteers creatively in the process, giving them "ownership" of the project and its outcome.

- **Form a public speaking outreach team**: Recruit and train volunteers to carry your fundraising message and "ask" into their place of worship or any civic organizations they are affiliated with. While the volunteer who sets up the event should make the presentation, you might want to team them with a trained fund raiser for support when it comes time to ask for the contribution.

- **Form a telephone response team:** The members of this team will be assigned to call and thank donors after a donation has been received and recorded. An orientation session should be held to set up the basic thank you message, which will then be personalized by the volunteer based on the material he or she receives about the donor.

- The call should accomplish two things: It should make the donor feel appreciated, and it should reassure the donor he or she has made a good decision by reinforcing their belief the organization is a good steward and is accomplishing meaningful work.

- To make these calls truly effective, ask the fund raisers who received the pledges or donations to make notes on the individual or the donation that will help the volunteer who calls at a later date personalize his or her call. One of the major reasons donors give for not renewing donations is the impersonal way they were thanked.

- **Form a team to write thank you notes**: This is a variation of the telephone team above. The notes can be handwritten or computer generated. Again, the basic message should be determined in collaboration with someone privy to campaign policy, but each note should be personalized for the donor. In smaller organizations the thank you can go out under the volunteer's name. Larger organizations led by someone known in the community may want their board chair or executive director to sign the letters.

- **Form a matching funds team**: This team will check with the organization's volunteers to see if any of them work with a company that might match employee donations. Have the team create an information packet out of campaign literature for these employees to take to their management. The employee or a trained fund raiser can ask the appropriate company executive to make the commitment, and request permission to tell employees about the fundraising campaign and volunteer opportunities available with the organization.

- **Form a friends and family contact team:** Take advantage of your volunteers' enthusiasm for your organization and mission and their personal social network. Form a team that will brainstorm ideas on how they can carry your fundraising campaign into their neighborhood communities and raise money from their neighbors and friends. Individual team members might hold small dinner parties or a neighborhood barbecue. If the volunteer is not comfortable asking for money, he or she can arrange to have an experienced fund raiser help with the presentation. Other ways they might raise funds for the campaign is to hold a carwash, put together a neighborhood garage sale, or arrange a competitive softball game between fathers and sons or the local police and fire departments. They can provide the legwork for getting campaign literature to local merchants.

- This kind of grassroots support can give your campaign visibility in areas your trained fundraisers have no time to cover and give you access to new donors and funds you would otherwise miss.

These are just some ideas to start you thinking about your volunteer talent and your fundraising needs and how best to use the one to meet the other.

Cultivating Home-Grown Fundraising Talent

Just because someone has never raised funds does not mean they cannot or do not want to become a fund raiser. Perhaps no one has ever given them the opportunity.

The advantage of recruiting your fund raisers from volunteers presently working with your organization is these candidates already have a relationship with your nonprofit. They know and are supportive of your mission. They recognize the qualities in your organization that make it special because they are the qualities that drew them to volunteer with you. By providing these volunteers with an opportunity to add fund raising to their volunteer experience, you strengthen the bond they have already built with your organization.

"Volunteers are effective fundraisers because their personal commitment to the organization's mission makes them convincing advocates for the cause. In addition, volunteers are likely to donate to the organization at which they serve."

— Stanford Social Innovation Review

One way to harvest this potential fundraising talent is to institute an on-going training program for volunteers interested in learning how to become fund raisers. Because personal growth is a major reason people volunteer, a program that teaches fundraising essentials such as how to communicate clearly and listen actively, how to plan and organize, and how to motivate people should be well received. The exercises involved in teaching these skills present an opportunity to make the course fun — another factor that will make the program appealing to your volunteers.

You can use a professional trainer for the course or an experienced fundraiser within your organization. There are many associations and organizations online that can provide assistance with the design of your program — sometimes at no cost. It is important that some members of your board take part in your training program. In addition to the valuable knowledge they have to share, and the enthusiasm for fundraising they can communicate, their involvement lets your volunteers know your organization is supportive of their decision to become involved in fundraising.

Once your volunteers feel comfortable with the skills they will learn and realize fundraising is about telling your story and making friends for your organization, you should have a reliable selection of qualified, well-trained fund raising candidates for your next capital campaign. But even if most of the volunteers who go through the program decide not to become involved directly in fundraising, your organization will still benefit.

Program participants will develop skills that will help with other types of volunteer assignments. Most importantly, the experience will increase their knowledge of your organization and their sense of involvement, which in most instances will translate to a deeper, longer volunteer commitment.

Volunteers as Donors

Is asking volunteers who donate their time to also donate money a form of "double dipping"? Susan Ellis, in her article "Should We Ask Volunteers to Give Money On Top of Time?" points to this belief as a reason some nonprofit fund raisers do not approach their organization's volunteers for donations. Another reason given is people volunteer because they cannot afford to donate money. Neither of these assumptions holds up under scrutiny.

Volunteering time and donating money are two possible ways for people to support a nonprofit. One does not cancel out the other. In fact, according to research, people who volunteer are more generous when it comes to giving money to the charity they volunteer for than people who do not volunteer. This is understandable. When it comes to volunteering, familiarity breeds loyalty and emotional attachment. We are all more likely to give generously to a cause we know and care about than to one with which we have no connection.

Regarding the argument that people volunteer because they cannot afford to donate money, how do you then account for the retired executives, the up-and-coming young corporate managers, or the successful entrepreneurs who carve time out of their busy lives to volunteer? Of all the reasons volunteers give for volunteering, a lack of money is rarely, if ever, mentioned.

On the other hand, there are good reasons to give your volunteers an opportunity to contribute to your fundraising campaign. It is a well-accepted axiom in fundraising that, for credibility, any person who wishes to solicit donations must first be a donor. As you set up your program to involve your volunteers in your fundraising campaign, a personal donation needs to be a prerequisite for participation. The amount of the contribution is irrelevant. What matters is the volunteer believes strongly enough in the value of the campaign that he or she is willing to contribute toward its success. Without making this commitment, any dealings they may have with donors or potential donors would lack honesty.

Even if you choose not to involve your volunteers in your fundraising campaign, they still deserve the opportunity to participate through a donation. Failing to provide them with this opportunity is a breach of trust. It infers that, in spite of the service they have given your organization, you do not trust their commitment enough to risk rejection if you request a donation.

Creating an Opportunity for Volunteers to Donate

Ideally, the opportunity to donate should be presented to the volunteer face-to-face, by someone who knows and has worked with him or her, someone who can honestly thank the volunteer for the important contribution he or she has made to the success of the organization. After expressing this gratitude, the individual can inform the volunteer about the fundraising campaign and tell the volunteer that if he or she decides to make a donation, it would be no problem to forward it to the appropriate person. Or the volunteer can be directed to the person who accepts donations.

An opportunity can also be made available during a volunteer meeting. The campaign can be announced and envelopes can be handed out, which the volunteers can either fill and hand in or take home and send in at their conveniences. This approach gives volunteers an opportunity to donate while protecting their privacy and confidentiality.

With either of these approaches there is no confrontation or pressure. The volunteer is thanked for the contribution of time and talent he or she has already contributed to the organization, and is presented with opportunity to donate to the ongoing fundraising campaign. The decision of when and how much — or even if — to donate is left up to the volunteer.

A Final Word

The practice of some nonprofits to treat fundraising as a separate entity unrelated to the day-to-day pursuit of their mission does a great disservice to their volunteers because it prevents them from fully understanding the challenge the nonprofit faces. Only vaguely conscious of the critical role fundraising plays, these volunteers enthusiastically promote the organization's work, but not its need for financial support. They share the organization's story without showing people how they can become a part of that story by helping to fund the organization. This happens because the organization has failed to keep the importance of fundraising foremost in their volunteers' consciousness.

The relationship between volunteers and fundraising should be organic; the two are interdependent. Without fundraising there would be no organization to volunteer for. Without volunteers, the funds raised would not be sufficient for the organization to fulfill its mission. Even if it is not feasible for you to include all of your volunteers in your fundraising efforts, it would serve you and your volunteers well to include fundraising awareness as an important part of your orientation and ongoing volunteer training. Empowering your volunteers to advocate for you in this arena will enrich their volunteer experience and your fundraising efforts.

Some Tips for Involving Your Volunteers in your Fundraising Campaign

- Your board's experience and knowledge of fundraising makes them a valuable asset in training volunteers who are uninitiated in the ways of fundraising for assignments that can support your trained fund raisers.

- The advantage of recruiting and training current volunteers to be fund raisers is your candidates will already have a relationship with your organization, be supportive of its mission, and familiar with its history.

- By forming volunteers into support teams, you can delegate fundraising work that can increase the effectiveness of your campaign without overburdening your trained fund raisers.

- With limited training, you can create a telephone support team to make personalized thank you calls to new donors, which will let the donors know they are appreciated and confirm they have made a good decision in donating to your organization.

- A support team of bloggers can help you craft and post blogs that can generate excitement, spread news about your campaign, and garner support for your organization during your fundraising drive.

- A volunteer email support team can help create a message and provide names from their personal email address book for a major email outreach to promote the campaign and solicit donations.

- Social networking is quickly becoming a viable resource for nonprofit fundraising. By creating a team of volunteers who use social networking to create and post information instructing people how to contribute to your campaign, you can expand your campaign outreach to a whole new host of potential donors.

- A system of volunteer support teams enables you to mobilize volunteers to go into their communities and create events and activities that will raise your campaign's visibility in areas not covered by your trained fund raisers. Such undertakings as car washes, neighborhood barbecues, small dinner parties, softball games, and neighborhood garage sales can generate money and create new donors.

- One complaint donors voice when asked why they stopped giving to a nonprofit was the impersonal manner in which they were thanked. This pitfall can be avoided by mobilizing support teams of volunteers to personalize your organization's thank you notes and phone calls.

- By asking fund raisers to make a brief notation about a donor or a donation when they submit the donation for recording, you will be able to provide your telephone or letter-writing volunteers with the material they need to personalize their thank you.

- Reassure volunteers willing to host a fundraising dinner or barbecue that you can provide a trained fund raiser to assist if they feel uncomfortable asking for money.

- If you have already trained some of your volunteers to speak at churches and civic organizations, just refocus their message and have them speak to these groups about your fundraising campaign.

- One way to bring home the importance of your fundraising campaign is to tie it to the work your volunteer is currently doing. If they are working with clients, use the annual cost of keeping the program operating as an illustration of why your organization needs to raise money for the coming year. Point out if you do not succeed in raising the money you need, programs like this one may have to be cut back or eliminated. This puts a face on the figures.

- Grants are another way nonprofits sustain their programs. Grant writers can be hired, but it is worth determining whether current volunteers have some raw grant writing talent (or whether some grant writers who have been operating under your radar). If you find some good candidates, invest in them. There are numerous grant and proposal writing courses available online or through universities. Enroll your potential grant writers in one of these courses and then put them to work.

- Incorporate a fund raiser apprentice program. Pair up a volunteer interested in learning how to be a fund raiser with an experienced fund raiser, and let them work as an assistant for one campaign. Reinforce what they learn by sending them to one of the fundraising workshops put on by professional trainers, associations, or various nonprofit organizations.

- Consider forming a volunteer team to go out into the community and hold focus groups to update yourself on how your fundraising campaign is being received by potential donors and, if applicable, clients. Let the team work with someone versed in campaign policy to analyze the results and make suggestions on improving your presentation to get better results. This information can also be used to improve your efforts in your next capital campaign.

- Have a couple volunteers review your organization's fundraising history. Have them chart the history, add a few historic pictures of your organization, and post the finished product on the department bulletin board. Also scan it into your computer so it can be sent out as part of an email.

- Have each of your field fundraisers submit an interesting donor story. Create a team of volunteers with computer capabilities to select three to five of the best stories. Get permission from the donors to tell the stories, and send a volunteer out to get some pictures. Have your volunteer team produce an electronic fundraising campaign newsletter and send it out to volunteers, donors, and anyone else on your email list. You might also want to feature one of the stories on your website. If any of the stories prove to be sufficiently interesting to warrant broader community exposure, get one of your outreach volunteers to create a press release for the story and submit it to your local paper.

- Depending on the length of your campaign, you might want to consider a mid-campaign appreciation event. One of your volunteer support teams could stage the event and serve coffee and donuts or homemade cookies. A board member could give an update on the figures, and the fund raisers who have brought in the most money could be recognized and thanked.

- A team could be created to produce periodic campaign status reports complete with charts to be posted or emailed to all volunteers, and if appropriate, donors, clients, or agency partners.

- A team of volunteer campaign "go-for's" could be created. Members could be temporarily assigned to whatever fundraising committee or individual is presently in need of extra help.

- Review your list of potential donors with your volunteers and ask them if they have any additions they feel they could help contact.

- Offer an on-going volunteer fundraising training program.

- Make a contribution to your current fundraising campaign (in any denomination) a prerequisite for becoming involved in the campaign. Explain why this is important to give credibility to anyone who comes in contact with donors or potential donors.

- Be sure to be free with expressing your gratitude to anyone who helps with your campaign, regardless of the scope of their involvement.

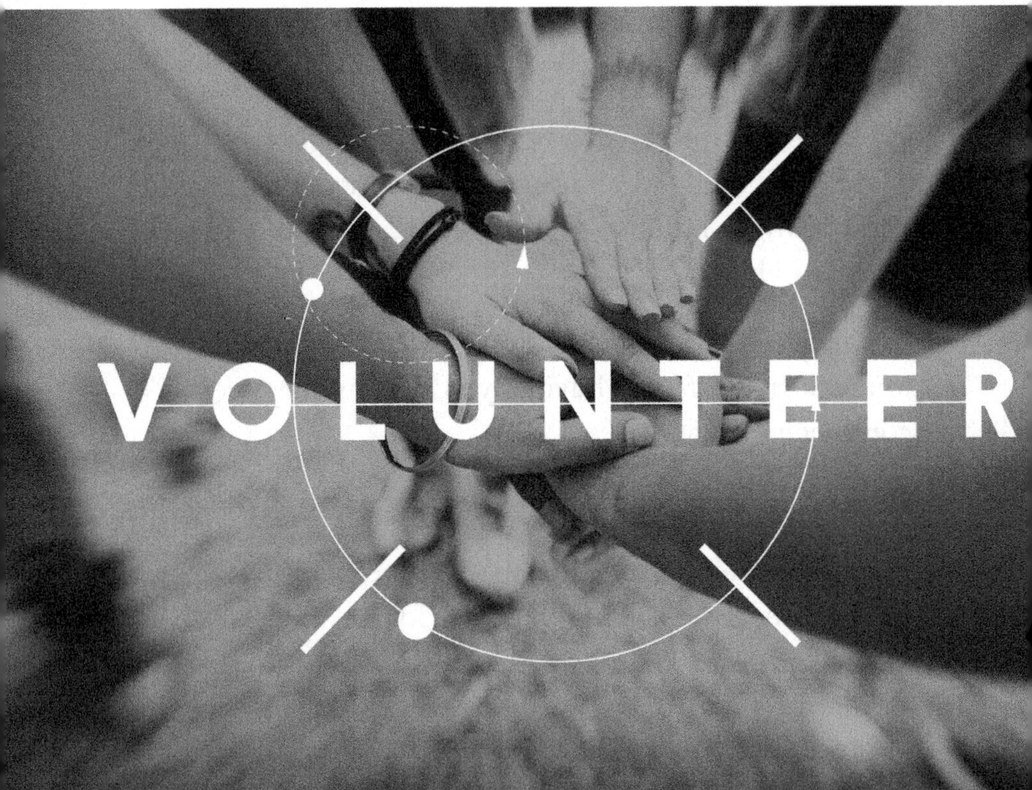
VOLUNTEER

CONCLUSION

We have focused on building a volunteer program that inspires long-term commitment, but we should clarify that term. This does not necessarily mean a continued period of service. Today many volunteers prefer to do their volunteering in brief segments, one project at a time, but very often for the same organization. This type of volunteering can also be built into a long-term commitment. A good example is the American Cancer Society engaging volunteers on the internet for small assignments sometimes requiring only minutes of the volunteer's time. But these volunteers come back again and again to provide valuable services to this organization.

If you can design short-term volunteer assignments to meet your needs that can be done either on-site or online, you can supplement your volunteer base with this new breed of volunteer. When cultivated properly, you can build a long-term relationship with these volunteers.

There are some common traits found in nonprofit organizations that have built successful volunteer programs. Regardless of their size or focus, they have all developed a culture of gratitude. They hold the traditional appreciation luncheons and dinners and recognition ceremonies, but their expressions of gratitude are not limited to these occasions. When they speak of their organization, their volunteers are always gratefully acknowledged. They are acknowledged in the organization's mission statement, and their value is made clear in employee training sessions. The invaluable role of volunteers is noted in all the organization's literature and mentioned on their website.

Another thing organizations with successful volunteer programs have in common is their commitment to motivate and empower their volunteers to succeed. This commitment informs the organizations' philosophies and policies. It is reflected in the way they recruit and the way they manage their volunteers.

And one other point: these organizations never lose sight of the fact that no matter how serious the reason is that motivated the individual to volunteer, every volunteer expects their experience to be enjoyable. These organizations weave an element of fun into their training, and all aspects of their program.

The secret to attracting and retaining quality volunteers will not be found in a list of motivational ideas or a compilation of ways to say thank you to volunteers, although these tools can be helpful. The truth is: there is no secret. Your success in recruiting and retaining volunteers hinges on the attitude you bring to the task, and the commitment you are willing to make to see your volunteers succeed in accomplishing whatever it was they volunteered to accomplish. In the end, it is the quality of the partnership you establish with your volunteers and how enjoyable you make their volunteer experience that will determine how well they serve you, and the length of their commitment.

Acknowledgements

This is a book of shared wisdom. It could never have been written without the help of the many individuals who graciously allowed me to tell their stories and explore their philosophy on recruiting and managing volunteers. While their official titles and the size and nature of their organizations vary, they have all expressed to me an abiding appreciation of volunteers, and a commitment to make the volunteer experience meaningful and rewarding for anyone willing to give of their time and talents.

My thanks to *Danielle Kearney*, Lutheran Services, Florida; *Jane Lowe*, Winthrop P. Rockefeller Cancer Institute, Arkansas; *Curtis Hammond*, Missoula Aging Services, Montana; *Barbara Price*, Thrivent Financial for Lutherans Habitat for Humanity Program, Washington; *Susan Jaye-Kaplan*, Link to Libraries, Massachusetts; *Mike Wahl*, Wauconda Illinois Cert Program; *Barbara Howard*, Bird Steward Program, Tampa Bay, Florida; *Sally Wilson*, "Yes Magazine," Washington ; *Ami Simms*, The Alzheimer's Art Quilt Initiative, Michigan; *Marisa Albanese*, Union Station Homeless Services, California; *Halle Tecco*, Yogabear.org, California; *Lori Tsuruda*, People Making A Difference, Massachusetts; *Barbara Goldman*, Executive Director emeritus, Santa Fe Rape Crisis and Trauma Treatment Center, New Mexico; *Norma H. Gurba*, former director, City of Lancaster Museum /Art Gallery, California, and *David Geary*, founder and former director, Universal Studio's Volunteer Disaster Response Teams, California. Their experiences have not only provided us with insight into the complex issues that confront volunteer managers, but have also presented us with solutions for some of these challenges.

I would also like to thank *Sarah Kassman*, Shanti Orange County,

California; *Lawrence Becerra*, Las Companas Compadres, New Mexico; *Breda Turner*, St. Vincent Health System, Arkansas; *Jane Davis*, Hope-Howse, New Mexico; *Brian Wagner*, The ARC Angels, Michigan, *Ruthe Coleman*, Santa Fe Symphony Orchestra, New Mexico, and *"Woody" Carlson*, Thrivent Financial for Lutherans Habitat for Humanity Program, Washington, who provided invaluable information for this book.

My special thanks to *Lauren Perlmutter*, March of Dimes, *Aubry Morgan and Laura Reeves*, The American Cancer Society, and *Robert Rosenthal* who generously shared their extensive knowledge of the rapidly changing nature of today's volunteerism, and how their organizations are meeting this new challenge. And I would like to thank Pamela Hawley, *Universal Giving*, for walking me through the new on-line face of today's volunteerism and for sharing what she has learned working in this computerized aspect of recruiting and placing volunteers in an international arena.

There are four other people I would like to thank — four generous professional trainers and consultants whose extensive work in the field greatly impacted the nature of this book: *Susan Ellis*, president of Energize, Inc., a training, consulting, and publishing firm that specializes in volunteerism; *Jayne Cravens*, an internationally-recognized consultant in communications, volunteer involvement and capacity-building for nonprofit and non-governmental organizations; *Steve McCurley*, a renowned trainer and speaker on volunteer involvement, and *Tony Poderis*, a consultant and lecturer on nonprofit fundraising. You can learn more about the resources offered by these individuals on their websites:

Susan Ellis: **www.energizeinc.com**

Jayne Cravens: **www.coyotecommunications.com**

Steve McCurley: **www.e-volunteerism.com/team/mccurley.php**

Tony Poderis: **www.raise-funds.com**

And finally, I would like to express my appreciation of the people for whom this book has been written — the men and women who have taken on the demanding and complex job of managing volunteers.

It is said that volunteers are the life-blood of a nonprofit organization, but in reality the value of any organization's volunteers depends on how they are managed. It takes considerable skill to do this well — to be able to assesses the talents and coordinate the time a volunteer brings to an organization, and direct the services of that volunteer in a manner that advances the organization's mission and also fulfills the volunteer's desire for personal growth and fulfillment through service.

The job requires a visionary, someone capable of seeing beyond the limitations frequently imposed by insufficient budgets and overwhelming logistics to recognize the unlimited potential of volunteers. A volunteer manager must be versatile. He or she will be called upon to fill many roles: that of recruiter, organizer, supervisor, cheerleader, bookkeeper, counselor, mediator, and — on occasion — miracle worker. And as they juggle all these responsibilities, they are expected to remain upbeat and model for their volunteers the enthusiasm and faith needed to accomplish the organization's mission. It is my hope that these men and women will find the shared wisdom in this book to be a useful tool in their day-to-day efforts to meet these challenges.

Bibliography

Bien, Adrienne, *15 Ways to Increase Volunteer Commitment*, **www.acei.org/15waystoincreasevolunteerism.doc.**

Building Active Citizens: The Role of Social Institutions in Teen Volunteering. Brief 1 in the *Youth Helping America* series, Washington, DC, November 2005.

Burnett, John J., *Nonprofit Marketing: Best Practices.*

Checco, Larry, *Five Ways to Protect Your Ethics and Preserve Your Brand*, **http://nonprofit.about.com/od/ nonprofitpromotion/fr/branding.htm.**

Clubine, Betsy, and Sarah Jane Rehnborg, *Volunteer Recruitment: Tips from the Field*, **www.serviceleader.org.**

Clubine, Betsy, and Sarah Jane Rehnborg, *Volunteer Tips from the Field*, **www.serviceleader.org.**

Conflict Resolution, Corporation for National and Community Service, **http://nationalserviceresources.org/practices/ topic/150.**

The Corporation for National and Community Service (CNCS), **www.nationalservice.gov**.

Cravens, Jayne, *Myths About Online Volunteering*, **www. coyotecommunications.com.**

Dos and Don'ts of Volunteer Recruiting, **www.nptimes.com.**

Dunlap, Patrick, and Judy Esmond, *Developing the Volunteer Motivation Inventory to Assess the Underlying Motivational Drive of Volunteers in Western Australia*, **www. morevolunteers.com/resources/MotivationFinalReport.pdf.**

Ellis, Susan J., *From The Top Down.*

Ellis, Susan J., *Look Back to Look Ahead Project,* **www. energizeinc.com/backahead.html.**

Ellis, Susan J., *The Volunteer Recruitment Book.*

Ellis, Susan J., *Why People Volunteer,* **www.serviceleader.org/ new.**

Enhancing Staff Volunteer Relationships: Handling Conflict, The Art of Volunteer development, **https://heritage.utah.gov/wp-content/uploads/am_resources_publication_art_volunteer. pdf?51f9e0.**

Enhancing the Volunteer Experience: Understanding, Motivation, and Commitment, **https://heritage.utah.gov/wp-content/ uploads/am_resources_publication_art_volunteer. pdf?51f9e0.**

Esmond, Judy, *Count Me In: 501 ideas on Recruiting Volunteers.*

Fact Sheet: Designing Effective Volunteer Positions, Points of Light Foundation, **http://pointsoflight.org.**

A Friendly Atmosphere for your Volunteers, **http://centreonphilanthropy.com/files/kb_ articles/1250259770Friendly%20Atmosphere%20for%20 Volunteering.pdf.**

Fritz, Joanne, *E-mail Tips to Your Board Members During a Major Gifts Campaign,* **http://www.about.com.**

Fritz, Joanne, *Five Steps to Defining your Nonprofit Brand,* **http://nonprofit.about.com/od/nonprofitpromotion/fr/ branding.htm.**

Fritz, Joanne, *Recruiting Volunteers - Three Approaches,* **http:// www.about.com.**

Fritz, Joanne, *Top 6 facts about youth volunteers,* The Journal of Volunteer Administration, Volume 22, Number 3, 2004.

Fritz, Joanne, *What Do Volunteers Want: 10 Ways to Make Volunteers Happy,* **http://nonprofit.about.com/od/volunteers/ tp/whatvolunteerswant.htm.**

Graff, Linda L., *Beyond Police Checks.*

The Health Benefits of Volunteering: Review of Recent Research, **www.nationalservice.gov.**

Holland, D.K., *Branding for Nonprofits.*

Independent Sector, **www.independentsector.org.**

Interviewing and Screening Volunteers, **www.energizeinc.com.**

Johnston, Alicia, A Strategic Guide to Social Media for Nonprofits, **http://sproutsocial.com/insights/nonprofit- social-media-guide.**

Katzekbach, Jon R., and Douglas K. Smith, *The Wisdom of Teams: Creating the High-Performance Organization.*

Lipp, John, *A Volunteers Bill of Rights,* **www.energizeinc.com.**

Little, Helen, *Volunteers: How to Get Them, How to Keep Them,* Panacea Press, Inc., Naperville, IL, 1999.

Lockhard, Pamela, *The Truth About Baby Boomers and Social Media,* July 1, 2015, **https://www.dmn3.com/dmn3-blog/ boomers-and-social-media.**

Luchuk, Louise Chatterton, *Best Practices in Staff and Volunteer Relations*, Charity Village Newsweek, April 26, 2004.

Lynch, Rick, and Steve McCurley, *How to Generate Conflict Between Volunteers and Staff*, CASA.Net Resources.

Lynch, Rick and Steve McCurley, *Volunteer Management.*

Lysakowski, Linda, *Nonprofit Essentials: Recruiting and Training Fundraising Volunteers.*

McCurley, Steve, *Building understanding and collaboration: creating synergistic relationships between staff and volunteers*, The Points of Light Foundation, Washington, DC, 1995, p. 3.

McCurley, Steve, and Sue Vineyard, *Handling Problem Volunteers.*

McKee, Thomas W., *Creating a High Commitment Volunteer Culture*, **www.volunteerpower.com/articles/HighCommitment.asp.**

McKee, Thomas W., *Recruiting and Managing Younger Volunteers*, www.volunteerpower.com/articles/GenX.asp.

McKee, Thomas W., *How to Motivate Volunteers*, **www.volunteerpower.com/articles/motivate.asp.**

McLeish, Barry J., *Successful Marketing Practices for Nonprofits.*

Merril, Mary V., *Interviewing Potential Volunteers for Specific Jobs*, September 2005, **www.worldvolunteerweb.org.**

Molitor, Douglas, *Branding for Nonprofits.*

Morrison, Emily Kittle, *Leadership Skills Developing Volunteers for Organizational Success.*

Nanji, Ayaz, *How Baby Boomers Use the Web, Social Networks, and Mobile,* July 18, 2013, **www.marketprofs.com.**

Nissim, Bill, *Nonprofit branding: Unveiling the Essentials,* October 2004, **www.ibranz.com, www.energizeinc.com.**

Ohio State University, *Conducting Volunteer Interviews: A Guide for Extension Educator,* **www.ohio4h.org.**

Poderis, Tony, *Fundraising Forum: How To Recruit Your Fundraising Team,* **www.raise-funds.com/1999/how-to-recruit-your-volunteer-fund-raising-team.**

Points of Light Foundation, *Effective Relationships Between Staff and Volunteers,Changing the Paradigm: Volunteer involvement self assessment kit,* Washington, D.C.

Recruitment and Organization of Volunteers, July 2007, **http://volunteertoday.com.**

Reid, Russ, **www.russreid.com.**

Rodriguez, Santiago, *Diversity and Volunteerism: Deriving Advantage from Difference,* **www.energizeinc.com.**

Sanborn, Mark, *Teambuilt: Making Teamwork Work.*

Scheier, Ivan H., *Building Staff/Volunteer Relations.*

State of the Sector Survey 2015, Nonprofit Finance Fund, **www.nonprofitfinancefund.org/state-of-the-sector-surveys.**

Virtual Volunteering Resources, **www.serviceleader.org/virtual.**

Volunteer Recruitment, American Association of Community Theater, **www.aact.org.**

Volunteering in America: 2007 State Trends and Rankings in Civic Life, Washington, DC, 2007.

Zeff, Robin, *Nonprofit Guide to the Internet*, **www.energizeinc. com/art.html.**

Additional Resources

The Electronic Gazette for Volunteerism:_

www.volunteertoday.com

Free help in setting up Risk Management and Liability Reduction Plans:

http://nonprofitrisk.org/tools/volunteer/volunteer.shtml

http://managementhelp.org/risk_mng/risk_mng.htm

www.primacentral.org/content.cfm?sectionid=196

DISC Model- Emotional and Behavioral Profiles:

https://internalchange.com

www.discprofiles4u.com/pages/About-DiSC-Profiles.html

www.onlinediscprofile.com/?gclid=CN3zg-KWupwCFSm8sgodsXlKXQ

www.discprofile.com

Complete Volunteer Policy Relationships Document from Vancouver Island Health Authority:

www.viha.ca/NR/rdonlyres/F5555952-A5C5-4EB3-9AC0-0AE6 215649AB/12703/5113Volunteer_Staff_Relations_vXXX1.pdf

Free articles on diversity trends:

www.diversitytrends.com/free_diversity_articles/index.html

Nonprofit Volunteer Commitment Form (sample):

www.openmedicinefoundation.org/wp-content/

uploads/2014/05/Sample-Volunteer-Commitment-Form.pdf

Tips for Creating Your Own Print Media:

10 Top Tips for Designing Your Own Business Cards, **https://design.tutsplus.com/articles/10-top-tips-for-designing-your-own-business-cards--cms-25539**

How to Design a Business Card: 10 Top Tips, **www.creativebloq.com/graphic-design/how-design-business-card-10-top-tips-9134291**

Free templates from inkd.com, **http://inkd.com/templates/free-templates**

Training Module 9: Handling Volunteer Performance Problems:

www.energizeinc.com/store/4-229-E-1

Glossary

Active listening: A communication technique that requires a listener to establish eye contact, stay focused, ask insightful questions, take appropriate action, and remember what is said.

Baby Boomers: Those born in the period following World War II.

Buddy System: Pairing a new volunteer with an experienced volunteer.

Blog: A frequently updated web page or website, run by a small group or an individual, that is written in a casual style.

Brand: A particular image or identity often considered a valuable asset to an individual or group.

Confidentiality policy: A principle of action proposed by an individual or group to keep someone's information private.

DiSC Model: A tool that evaluates a person's behavior by focusing on four different traits: dominance, inducement, submission, and compliance.

Grassroots: An organization's most basic level, often comprised of regular people regarded as the main body of membership.

Press Release: An official statement issued by an individual or organization that provides information on a certain matter.

Recruitment campaign: The procedure of looking and finding people to join an organization.

Recruitment package: Materials given to volunteers that spell out an organization's history, specific needs, and contact information.

Social Media: Websites and other forms of electronic communication through which users create content, connect with online communities, and exchange information.

Index

About the Author

Born in Colorado, Angela Erickson married a handsome Texan and spent 10 years living down in the South before recently moving back to her home state. She and her husband Kyle spent seven years fostering children in the state of Texas and have adopted four — three girls and a boy. Putting that double major from college to good use, she has served as a middle school teacher and as a youth director at two churches, helping to train and oversee volunteers for youth, children, and family programs. Angela loves reading, writing, music, running, and spending time with family and friends. She is borderline addicted to puttering around on ancestry.com and is also an enthusiastic anglophile.

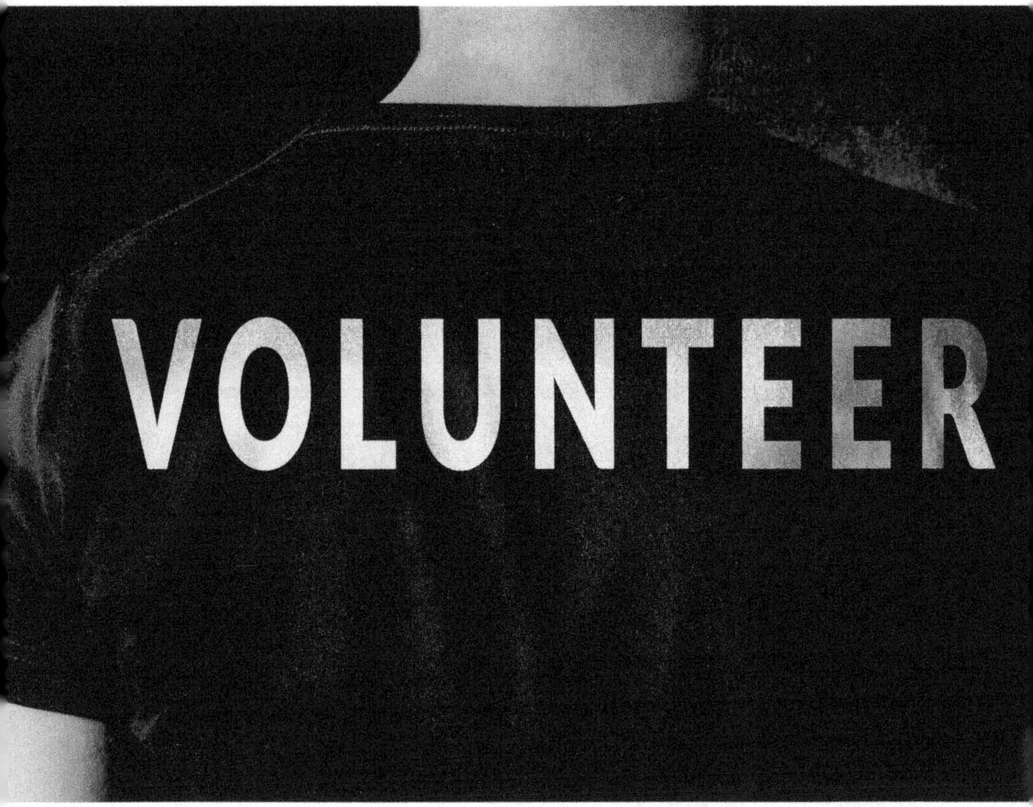
VOLUNTEER